The Author

A successful businessman as well as an historian and educator, Warren B. Smith went from an Eastern preparatory school to a Chicago High School before entering the University of Chicago in the spring of 1897. He received the Ph.B. degree in June, 1902, in the meantime having worked at the bench in a shoe factory, in a wholesale merchandise house, and as a sales correspondent. He served an eighteen months' apprenticeship learning to cast brass, before entering the real estate business with his father in Chicago in 1904.

He took correspondence courses in history and in January, 1910, returned to the University of Chicago as a graduate student in history and political science. From September, 1912, until February, 1916, he was in charge of the history department of Ripon (Wisc.) College. His father's death made it necessary for him to return to their business in Chicago. In 1918 he was "drafted" by the University of Chicago to teach European history, which was required of all new Army officer-inductees. This gave him the opportunity to complete residence requirements for his Ph.D.

Mr. Smith is still in the real estate business in Chicago and is a guiding spirit of the building and loan association organized by him in 1924 and chartered as a federal savings and loan association in 1934.

He has indeed led a busy life and has results to show for it. But this isn't all—he is, as he says, again "hunting" scholastically, when well past the age of eighty-two.

WHITE SERVITUDE

in

Colonial South Carolina

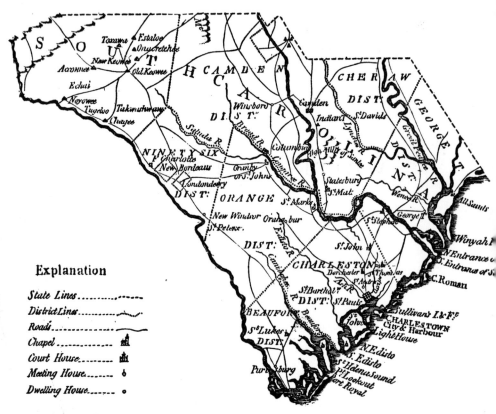

Explanation

State Lines .... ·-----
District Lines .... ~·
Roads .... —
Chapel .... 🏛
Court House .... 🏛
Meeting House .... ♭
Dwelling House ...... °

Map of South Carolina, By J. Denison, from Rev. Jedidiah Morse's Universal Geography

WHITE SERVITUDE

in

Colonial South Carolina

by

Warren B. Smith

UNIVERSITY OF SOUTH CAROLINA PRESS

COLUMBIA   1961

CONTENTS

TABLES

ILLUSTRATIONS

INTRODUCTION

In 1911, WHILE I WAS A GRADUATE STUDENT, majoring in history at the University of Chicago, Dr. Marcus W. Jernegan recommended to me, as a possible subject for my doctoral thesis, "White Servitude in Colonial South Carolina."

Authoritative monographs which dealt with the presence of such an institution in colonies to the north had already appeared. In 1895 Ballagh had made a study of the institution in Virginia;[1] in 1896 Bassett had done the same for North Carolina;[2] in 1901 Geiser for Pennsylvania;[3] and in 1904 McCormac for Maryland.[4]

Ballagh had dismissed white servitude in colonies to the south with the remark that "Georgia and the Carolinas also encouraged the importation of servants of the better class."[5] Bassett summed up his findings in the following words: "As for the indented servants . . . they never were a serious factor in the history of the colony. They came into it along with the earliest settlers, but the acceptance of slavery in Virginia had already sealed their fate."[6] Geiser, in his review of McCormac's work, wrote: "Dr. McCormac's work may be said practically to complete the history of the institution of indentured service in America." This remark he backed up by adding that "Virginia, Pennsylvania, and Maryland were the great servant-importing colonies."[7] A. Maurice Low summed up the work in this field by writing: "In Virginia and Maryland, great as the evils of slavery were in degrading free white labor, there was still room for the white indented servant and the freeman, but in South Carolina that was impossible."[8]

One perceptive student of South Carolina history had tried in October 1911 to refute Low's statement that having white indentured servants in South Carolina was an impossibility. Theodore Jervey presented as evidence of the existence of the institution the fact that thirty-two Scottish servants had been purchased in 1716 by the governor for the protection of the frontier.[9] However, when Elizabeth Donnan was investigating the subject in 1920, she went back to the Bassett thesis that white indentured servants had been brought in originally but had been outnumbered very soon by the slaves. She used as evidence of the growing black population the fact that in 1698 an act for the "Encouragement of the Importation of White Servants" had been passed which was designed to maintain the same balance between Negroes and white servants as had existed in the first years of the colony.[10]

It is apparent that those who have ignored the white servant element have always thought in terms of the black majorities of a later date, when rice had become the great staple of the colony. What they have overlooked is the fact that although rice was steadily growing in favor, the eighteenth century was almost half over before it became the major agricultural product, demanding more and more Negroes as methods were devised that vastly increased the output of that product.

Late in 1915, while I was Professor of History at Ripon College, a third draft of my thesis was submitted to Dr. Jernegan, who advised that it needed only a sufficiently comprehensive concluding chapter. In February 1916 circumstances obliged me to return to the business world, where I have been active ever since. Forty years had passed when a routine letter of inquiry put me in touch with Dr. J. Harold Easterby, late Director of the South Carolina Archives Department, at Columbia. Because of the encouragement offered by him, by Dr. Robert L. Meriwether, late Director of the South Caroliniana Library, and by Dr. Anne King Gregorie, late Editor of the *South Carolina Historical Magazine,* I have returned to my task. A bit to my surprise, I find the matter just about where I had left it.

In 1929 Dr. Arthur Henry Hirsch (who was one of my fellow students in 1913) published *The Huguenots in Colonial South Carolina.* He stuck to the traditional interpretation and doubted the real importance of the white servants. He admitted that "white servitude was coeval with the period of the first permanent settlement" but added that "there is, however, no evidence that a large number of Huguenots went to Carolina as servants.[11] He was, of course, dealing with a special subject.

There is still no direct treatment of the subject, although some of the historians more recently have seen a need for a revision of the earlier statements. Two very helpful books have added greatly to a renewed interest in this study. In 1929 appeared Verner W. Crane's *The Southern Frontier, 1670-1732,* and in 1940 Robert L.

Meriwether's *The Expansion of South Carolina, 1729-1765.* Early work in South Carolina history had centered on Charleston but these books filled a great void by treating the upcountry world. The first is a graphic portrayal of the vastness of what really was the colony's far-reaching frontier, and the second pursued the actual annexation of the upcountry, step by step. At the very beginning of his work, Dr. Meriwether pointed to "the favorite measure of the Proprietary period" as "forced employment of indentured servants on the plantations." [12]

In 1947 Abbott Emerson Smith's *Colonists in Bondage* was published. As he made use of sources in England, additional material on South Carolina might have been expected. However, his references to South Carolina are few and he sticks to the general view that South Carolina was "the only continental colony in which Negro labor was wholly preferred to white." [13] Perhaps it was the general nature of the work covering all of the colonies that prevented him from dipping more deeply into the sources.

A debt of gratitude is owed to Dr. Richard Walsh, whose volume entitled *Charleston's Sons of Liberty* was published in 1959. This is "A Study of the Artisans (1763-1789)." The outbreak of the American Revolution had been the end of the period under study, when first this history of indentured servants was undertaken. Inspiration came from Dr. Walsh's volume to suggest the possible interest of former servants as citizens-in-the-making of the new American nation.

A thesis to disprove a generally accepted idea has held great appeal. I am still sanguine enough to believe that the testimony I shall produce will prove my point: not that there were as many indentured servants in South Carolina as there were in Virginia and Maryland, but that they did constitute an important factor in the growth of the colony.

—WARREN B. SMITH

December 1960.

WHITE SERVITUDE
in
Colonial South Carolina

CHAPTER I

The Introduction of White Indentured Servants

THE PROVINCE OF CAROLINA WAS SETTLED more than sixty years after Virginia and forty years after Barbados. It was natural that the land of rice should fall heir to some of the institutions of the land of tobacco and the land of sugar. Negro slaves had been introduced into Virginia in 1619, but by 1649 their number had increased only to 300. In 1670, the year of the first settlement on the banks of the Ashley, there were in Virginia but 2,000 slaves.[1] Virginia had not, therefore, at the time of the first settlements in Carolina, definitely decided in favor of Negro slaves. In the West Indian colonies, while the superiority of Negro labor had already been demonstrated,[2] white servants were still used in large numbers, even in the field work of the plantations.[3] And the new colony, whose beginnings fell in the period when the use of white servants was perhaps at its height, naturally took very kindly to such labor.

The first fleet to sail for Carolina stopped at the island of Barbados to pick up men and supplies. Thus many of the first settlers of Carolina came from Barbados. In the proposals of the Barbados men to settle in Carolina can be found the statement: "There are many hundreds of noble families and well experienced planters that are ready to move speedily thither, with Negroes and servants."[4] The intimate relations between Barbados and the early settlements in South Carolina facilitated the adoption of usages customary in the older colony.

The public records of England indicate quite clearly that many white servants were sent to Barbados. In March 1655 the Council of State directed the Governor of Tynemouth Castle to certify the number of prisoners taken at Dunbar, that they might be sent to Barbados.[5] In August 1655 the Council of State ordered the transportation to Barbados of "all prisoners lately committed to the Marshalsea, who were taken in the Brest man-o-war."[6] In September 1655 the Council of State commanded "the Commissioners of the

[3]

Admiralty" to give orders "for those English, Scotch, Irish and Dutch mariners, prisoners in the castle of Plymouth . . . to be sent to Barbados." [7] In 1661 the council and assembly of Barbados passed an "Act for the Good Governing of Servants." [8] During the latter half of the seventeenth century a constant stream of petitions flowed home from Barbados requesting the sending out of white servants.[9] These facts are proof of the acceptance of the institution of white servitude by the Barbadians, and therefore indirectly by the first settlers of South Carolina. It would not be unreasonable to expect that among the Carolina immigrants were some who were already serving indentures and inured to the conditions of such servitude.

This is not merely a matter of inference. Proof can be found in the passenger list of the "Carolina," one of the three ships that sailed for Carolina from England in 1699. In this ship there were sixteen passengers who brought a total of sixty-three servants as well as thirteen passengers who had no servants. The complete list of names follows:

CAPT SULLIVAN

Ralph Marshall
Rich: Alexander
Tho Kinge
Eliz: Mathews

James Montgomery
Stephen Wheelwright
Eliz Dommocke

STEP BULL

Robert Done
Tho Ingram
John Larmouth

Barnaby Bull
Jonathan Barker
Dudley Widgier

ED HOLLIS AND JOS DALTON

George Prideox
Henry Price
John Dawson
Alfred Harleston
Susanna Kinder

Thomas Younge
Will. Chambers
Will Roades
Jane Lawson

THO AND PAULE SMITH

Aice Rixe
Jo. Burroughs
Eliz: Smith
Francis Noone

Jo Hudlesworth
Hugh Wigleston
Andrew Boorne

HAMBLETON (JNO HAMILTON)

Tho Gourden	Will Lumsden
Jo Frizen	Step Flinte
Edw Young	Jo Thomson
Samuel Morris	Tho Southell
Agnis Payne	Jo. Reed

JO RIVERS

Tho Poole	Rob. Williams
Henry Burgen	Math Smallwood

NICH CARTWRIGHT

Tho Gubbs	Jo Loyde
Martin Dedson	Step Price
Will Jenkins	

MORRIS MATHEWS

Alva Phillips	Reginold Barefoot
Mathew Hewitt	Eliz Currie

WILL BOWMAN

Abraham Smith	Millicent How

DOCTOR WILL SCRIVENER

Margaret Tudor

WILL OWENS

John Humphreys	Christopher Swade
John Borley	

THO MIDDLETON-ELIZ. uxor ejus

Rich Wright	Tho Wormes

SAMUEL WEST

Andrew Searle	Will West

JOSEPH BAILEY

John Carmichaell

PASSENGERS THAT HAVE NO SERVANTS

Mr. Tho Rideall	Mr. Will Houghton
Mr. Will Hennis	Mr. Tho Humfreys
Eliz Humphreys	Marie Clerke
Sampson Darkenwell	Nathanyell Darkenwell
Mrs. Sarah Erpe	Eliz Erpe
Martha Powell	Mrs. Mary Erpe [10]
Thomas Motteshed	

It is true that no statement is made as to the character of service to be rendered by these servants. Possibly some of the above were paid, personal servants, but the more likely presumption is that many of them were indentured servants. Just prior to the departure of this fleet the Proprietors had offered a head-right of 150 acres of land to every freeman coming out before March 25, 1670, plus 150 acres for every able manservant carried with him and 100 acres for every woman servant and for every manservant under 16. The amount of land to be granted for transporting servants was to be reduced each year for two consecutive years.[11] The greatest advantage therefore pertained to bringing servants to the Province during the first year.

The indenture of Millicent How, one of the sixty-three servants whose names appear on the passenger list of the "Carolina," was made out in London in September 1669. Her indenture reads: "Know all men that I Millicent How of London Spinster the day of the date hereof doe firmely by these pnts bind and oblige my selfe as a faithfull & obedient Sert in all things whatsoever, to serve and dwell with Capt. Joseph West of the sd City of London Merchant, in the plantation, or province of Carolina, according to the lawes & Customes and Orders for servts, wch are provided and settled in the said place; The said Joseph West providing for the sd Millicent his Servant all such necessarys in the time of her service and at the expiracon of her terme as the lawes and Orders of the place doth like wise provide and Oblidge Masters to pforme to their servnts. Wittnesse my hand and seale this pnt twentyeth day of September 1669."

Joseph West must have sold her services before the fleet sailed, for her name appears in the list as the servant of Will Bowman. The above indenture was signed by Millicent How, witnessed by

Stephen Bull, entered in the colonial records under date of September 8, 1671, and certified the same day by Joseph Dalton, secretary of the province.[12]

The "Carolina," still under the command of Henry Brain, returned in the fall of 1670 to Barbados to pick up a second load of colonists. Among these were indentured servants. Their names and the time that each had yet to serve were proved before Thomas Gray.

> Thomas Witty a sawyer is to serve two years.
> Thoas patterson a Carpenter is to serve two yeares.
> Richard poore a Sayer is to serve eighteene Monthes.
> John Cole a planter is to serve two yeares, six Monthes.
> Evan Howell a planter, serves two yeares, six Monthes.
> Moses fflower is to serve two yeares.
> John Croxton is to serve two yeares.
> Samll Buzard Taylor serves two yeares.
> Joan Burnet a woman servant serves three yeares.
> John Ratcliffe to serve two yeares.[13]

John Ratcliffe, the last named, developed a decided penchant for trouble making and occupied considerable space in the early records of the colony.[14] Indentured servants were among the earliest arrivals in Carolina, both from the Mother Country and from the islands.

The reasons for the introduction of white servants into South Carolina fall under three general heads: to aid in the settlement of the country, to meet the labor shortage, and to defend the colony. The initial need, of course, was for the settlement of the country. Shaftesbury and Locke had outlined for Carolina in their *Fundamental Constitutions* an intricately arranged feudal society. At the top were to be the Proprietors, holding one-fifth of the land; next the local nobility (landgraves and cassiques), holding one-fifth of the land; and finally the people, with the remaining three-fifths.[15] Yet even among the people the establishment of manors was possible. All would hold their lands of the Proprietors as the Proprietors held theirs of the Crown. The Proprietors were to pay annually twenty marks of silver to the Crown, while they in turn were to receive quitrents from their tenants. It should have been easy to obtain men to fill the upper ranks of these theoretical divisions, but the enlistment of a supporting population for this landed hierarchy was a more difficult task. The actual plan adopted for the solution of this problem had as its central idea acceptances by the grantees, as one of the conditions of the grant of land, of a distinct obligation to bring in or to send in settlers.

By Number 6 of the "Temporary Laws" of Carolina, promulgated in May 1671, all lords of baronies and manors were "to have each upon his barony 30 persons and upon his manor 15 persons respectively within seven years of the date of his grant, or be liable to a fine by the Parliament of Carolina, unless the Lords Proprietors allow him longer time." [16] A special obligation later attached to the 12,000-acre barony was that "within five years they build upon said colony one town to contain thirty houses, and four in each house." [17] A few years later the law was changed, requiring the grantees to "people at the rate of ten men for every 1,000 acres within five years, and bring over one-fifth of the number every year until the full number be completed." [18] Apparently the easiest way of meeting these obligations was to exploit those classes who, voluntarily or otherwise, joined the ranks of indentured servants.

Table I presents in order a list of the larger grants, those containing more than 1,000 acres, made during the early period (the seventeenth century) of Carolina's history. These items have been taken from the abstracts of such grants, as they appear in the Calendar of State Papers. These grants were made under the general conditions outlined above, although at time special conditions were made as indicated in the list.

TABLE I

17th Century Grants of More than 1,000 Acres

The first 15 are tabulated in the original documents; the balance of the list was compiled

Grantee	Acres	Comment	Date	CSP, Colonial
Lady Margaret Yeamans	1,070	On Yeaman's Creek	Feb. 9th, 1674	IX, 717
Earl of Shaftsbury	12,000	Ashley River	Mch. 18th, 1675	IX, 717
John Smyth	1,800	Ashley River	Nov. 25th, 1675	IX, 717
Sir Peter Colleton	12,000	Cooper River	Sep. 7th, 1677	X, 547
Sir Peter Colleton	4,423		Sep. 6th, 1679	X, 1249
Edward Middleton	1,000	On Goose Creek	Nov. 14th, 1680	X, 1638
P., Th. & Jas. Colleton	3,000	Cooper River	Mch. 5th, 1680	X, 1638
Sir Peter Colleton	4,420	Cooper River	Mch. 5th, 1680	X, 1638
Joseph West	1,500	Cooper River	Nov. 15th, 1680	X, 1638
Florentia O'Sullivan	2,400	Ashley River	July 6th, 1680	X, 1638
John Ashby	2,000	Cooper River	Apr. 25th, 1681	XI, 356
Joseph Thorowgood	3,000	Oolacoll Creek	Sept. 4th, 1682	XI, 879
Andrew Percivall	2,000	Ashley River	Jul. 26th, 1682	XI, 879
Stephen Fox	1,350	Stono River	Jun. 20th, 1682	XI, 879
Sir Peter Colleton	12,000	Cooper River	Feb. 12th, 1682	XI, 879
Jacob Waite (a Quaker)	12,000	To build a town of 30 houses, with 100 settlers in 5 years	Jun. 9th, 1675	IX, 577
Seth Sothell	12,000	Sothell same, ex—to produce 120 people	Jun. 11th, 1675	IX, 584
Mr. Beresford	3,000	40 settlers in 3 yrs.	May 17th, 1680	X, 1355
Christopher Smith	3,000	40 settlers in 3 yrs.	May 17th, 1680	X, 1355
George Warburton	3,000	40 settlers in 5 yrs.	Mch. 26th, 1681	XI, 54
Mr. Archdale, purchaser of Lady Berkeley's proprietorship	12,000		May 25th, 1681	XI, 119
Richard Banks	3,000	in "north part"	Aug. 6th, 1681	XI, 196

TABLE I—Continued

Grantee	Acres	Comment	Date	CSP, Colonial
Jno. Monke	1,000		Jul. 19th, 1682	I, 209*
William Shaw	3,000		Apr. 22nd, 1685	XII, 142
Jean de Genillat	3,000	"the first of the Swiss nation who has announced his intention of settling in Carolina"	Jul. 30th, 1685	XII, 295
James le Bas	3,000		Sep. 20th, 1685	XII, 373
Andrew Perceval	1,000		Oct. 1st, 1685	XII, 391
Josias Forrest	3,000		Mch. 2nd, 1686	XII, 588
Henry Augustus Chastaigner, Seigneur de Cramahe, and Alex. Thezée Chastaigner Seigneur de Lisle	3,000		Sep. 4th, 1686	XII, 842
Mons. John d'Arsens, Seigneur of Wernhaut	12,000		Oct. 29th, 1686	XII, 953
Maurice Matthews	3,000	"In consideration of his having purchased the lands from the Indians"	Nov. 2nd, 1686	XII, 961
James Mantell Goulard de Vervant.	3,000		Dec. 7th, 1686	XII, 1043
James Mantell Goulard de Vervant.	12,000		Dec. 7th, 1686	XII, 1044
Mr. John Price	40,000	Lords Proprietors to Governor Colleton: "We have agreed to grant to Mr. John Price forty thousand acres of land on certain letter of conditions herewith transmitted to you"	May 13th, 1687	XII, 1247
Dr. Christopher Dominick	12,000	"He having paid £600 for the same"	June 19th, 1688	XII, 1800
Thomas Smith	12,000		Dec. 9th, 1689	XIII, 629
James le Bas	1,800		Dec. 23rd, 1689	XIII, 653
Thomas Amy	12,000		Oct. 17th, 1694	XIV, 1420
James Boyd	3,000		Dec. 27th, 1694	XIV, 1622

In some instances land was granted unencumbered by such restrictions. In 1682 John Ashby was allowed an additional 3,000 acres because of "much good service in procuring seeds." [19] The following year a warrant was issued for 800 acres each to Mr. Francis Derowsery and Arthur Middleton, "though they bring no servants for the same, in consideration of their industry in the growth of wine in Carolina." [20] A warrant was also drawn for a grant of 3,000 acres to Monsieur Chavasse, "a person well skilled in drugs and other secrets of nature." [21]

There was also a system of land grants for the lesser folk who came out individually or in families, sometimes bringing a few servants with them. This head-right system granted 150 acres of land to every freeman coming out before March 25, 1670, with 150 acres more for every able manservant brought with him, 100 for every womanservant or manservant under 16, and 100 for every manservant after he had served his time. To those coming out before March 25, 1671, the grants were 100 and 70 respectively; and to those coming out before March 25, 1672, the grants were 70 and 60 respectively.[22] In 1679, because of "the remoteness of families one from another, by reason of the great tracts of land possessed by men who will not be able for a long time to stock them fully," the amounts were reduced to 70, 70, 50, and 60 acres.[23] In 1682 the plots were reduced still further in size to 50, 50, 50, and 40 acres.[24]

Grants, in pursuance of these offers, were made to Lords Proprietors themselves, to ship-captains, to immigrants with servants, to husbands for their wives, and to servants direct. In many cases, the bounty was divided among several interested parties. In some instances, the full bounty was granted to more than one party, for the bringing in of the same person. Table II illustrates the various angles at which the white servant touched the granting of lands.

TABLE II

Land-Grant Records of Early Carolina—with servants noted

Date of Grant	Grantee	Date of Arrival	Arriving a Servant	Self	Number of Servants	Acres	Page Number
5/21/72	Jas. Colleton et al	April/72			2	200	4
5/21/72	Stephen Bull	Aug./71			2	170	5
5/21/72	Stephen Bull	1st Fleet		x	2	400	6
5/21/72	Stephen Bull	April/71			1	100	6
5/21/72	Thos. & Jas. Smith	Aug./71			2	200	9
5/21/72		1st Fleet	Hy. Jones		1	100	9
5/21/72		1st Fleet	Hy. Jones		1	100	14
7/ 9/72	Sam. Boswood	Aug./71			1	70	19
7/27/72		1st Fleet	Wm. Bevin		1	100	21
7/27/72	Henry Hughes	1st Fleet		x &	½	225	22
7/27/72	John Coming*	1st Fleet	wife	x &	½	325	23
7/27/72	Richard Cole	1st Fleet		x &	2	450	23
7/27/72	Joseph Dalton	1st Fleet			7	1,150	24
7/27/72	John Williamson	1st Fleet		x	2	450	27
7/27/72	Samuel West	1st Fleet		x	2	450	27
8/28/72	Thomas Gray	June/71			7	700	28
8/30/72		1st Fleet	Dennis Mahoon		1	100	33
8/30/72		1st Fleet	Nath. Dartnell		1	100	34
9/ 7/72	Thomas Hurt	Aug./71		x	2	370	34
9/ 7/72		1st Fleet	Hugh Sherdon		1	100	35
9/ 7/72	Anthony Churn	1st Fleet	(for wife)		1	100	36
9/ 7/72	Fl. O'Sullivan	1st Fleet		x	12	1,900	37

Date	Name	Arrival	Notes		No.	Acres	No.
9/ 7/72	Fl. O'Sullivan	Aug./71			1	100	37
10/18/72	John Coming *	1st Fleet	wife	x &	½	375	45
11/23/72	John Coming *	Aug./71			5	570	45
11/23/72	Robert Goffe	July/72		x	1	200	48
11/23/72	Adm'r for Paul Smith and John Boon	1st Fleet		x	3	700	48
11/23/72	Thomas Buttler	Aug.,72		x	3	400	49
11/23/72	John Pinke	Feb.,71			1	100	51
11/23/72	Wm. Nath. Sayle *	1st Fleet	3 negroes & (in Jamestown)	x	2	1,300	52
11/23/72	Mrs. Gaud	Sept./70					
12/ 2/72	John Culpeper	Feb.,71					
		Dec./71	wife; slave	x	1	370	53
12/ 2/72	Mrs. Jane Robinson	Feb.,71		x	1	170	54
12/ 2/72	Capt. John Robinson	Feb.,71		x	1	200	54
12/ 7/72	Richard Cole	Aug.,71			8	800	55
12/ 7/72	Richard Deyos	1st Fleet		x	1	300	55
1/18/73		Feb./70	John Watkins		1	100	57
1/18/73		Feb./70	Thos. Archcraft		1	100	58
4/26/73	Mrs. Dorcas Smith	Feb./70	2 slaves	x		270	60
5/ 3/73		April/70	John May		1	100	60
3/ 2/73	Wm. Nath. Sayle *	1st Fleet	3 negroes & 1 near James Towne	x	2	1,050	61
		Sept./70					
5/10/73	Wm. Thomas	May/73	2 negroes "of" (servants)	x	3	270	61
			one a child		3	340	62
5/10/73	Coll. Joseph West	1st Fleet			2	200	62
		Aug./71			5	470	63

* Illegal grant

TABLE II—Continued

Date of Grant	Grantee	Date of Arrival	Arriving a Servant	Self	Number of Servants	Acres	Page Number
6/ 2/73	John Boon	Dec./71			1	70	63
1/28/75	Edw. Mathews	Aug./71			1	100	64
10/ 4/75		1st Fleet	Wm. Cockfield		1	100	65
11/24/73	Thomas Smith	Feb./72			1	70	66
1/27/74	Wm. Morrill	Aug./72	son	x	3	470	67
3/27/74	John ffallock	March/74	wife; 4 children	x	4	880	68
3/ 7/74	Thomas Hurt*	Aug./71			3	370	68
3/27/74		1st Fleet	Christopher Swaine		1	100	69
4/18/74	Capt. Stephen Bull*	E			2	400	70
4/18/74	Capt. Stephen Bull*	Aug./71			2	170	70
4/18/74	Capt. Stephen Bull*	April/71			1	100	70
4/18/74		1st Fleet	Thomas Worme		1	100	71
4/18/74		Dec./71	Philip Braidy		1	70	72
4/18/74	Mrs. Joane Carner	Aug./72	daughter; 1 negro	x		270	72
5/30/74	Thomas Lane	May/73			7	740	75
6/27/74	Amos Jefford	Dec./71			3	400	76
6/27/74		Dec./71	John Mills		1	70	77
6/27/74		Dec./71	James Hutton		1	70	77
7/25/74	Lt. Coll. John Godfrey	Feb./71			2	200	78
					1	100	78
9/ 5/74	John Cattell	Aug./72			1	70	82
9/ 5/74	Lady Margarett Yeamans	1671	"soe many servants and negroes"	x	?	1,070	82
9/ 5/74	Henry Hughes*	1st Fleet		x	½	225	82

[14]

Date	Name	Arrival	Note		No.	Acres	Page
9/ 5/74	Lt. Coll. John Godfrey	1671-1672	"soe many negroes and servants"	x	1	200	83
9/ 5/74	Simon Berringer	June/71		x	?	3,000	84
9/ 5/74	Oliver Spencer	Aug./72			4	340	84
		Aug./72		x	1	200	84
9/ 5/74		Feb./70	Thos. Machanelloe		1	70	85
5/30/74		1st Fleet	John Cole		1	70	85
9/ 5/74	John Berringer	1672-1673	"soe many servants"		…	:	86
9/ 5/74	Mrs. Dorcas Smith	Dec./71	1 negro	x	2	340	87
11/10/74	Capt. Richard Conant	June/71	and 1 negro	x	:	150	89
11/10/74	John Pinckett	1st Fleet	wife; son	x	1	360	90
12/21/74	Capt. Stephen Bull *	1st Fleet			1	100	91
12/ 5/74		Feb./72	Jas. Wms. & wife *		2	200	91
3/20/75	Amos Jefford	Aug./71			1	100	95
4/12/75	Thos. & Jas. Smith *	1st Fleet			2	200	96
4/12/75	Thos. & Jas. Smith *	1670-1671			4	550	96
4/27/75	Lt. Coll. Godfrey *	…1670	wife	x	1	300	97
4/27/75	Lt. Coll. Godfrey *	1st Fleet	2 sons	x	3	440	97
12/ 5/75		Feb./72	Jas. Wms. & wife *		2	200	99
9/ 4/75		Sept./75	William Long		1	70	101
9/14/75	Jacob Wayte	1st Fleet	wife; son	x	3	600	104
9/14/75	Capt. F. O'Sullivan *	Aug./71		x	12	1,900	104
9/14/75	Capt. F. O'Sullivan *				1	100	105
10/16/75	John Smith		wife	x	7	870	105
11/27/75	Thomas Dickison	Sept./75		x	1	200	108
12/10/75	Robert Browne	Aug./72			3	500	110
12/10/75	Thomas Butler	Sept./75	wife; 2 children	x	2	410	112

* Illegal grant

[15]

TABLE II—*Continued*

Date of Grant	Grantee	Date of Arrival	Arriving a Servant	Self	Number of Servants	Acres	Page Number
9/ 5/74	Margaret Lady Yeamans	Aug./72	8 negroes	x	1	880	112
9/ 5/74	Margaret Lady Yeamans	Feb./74					
2/19/76	Edw. Mathews	Aug./71		x	5	570	113
2/19/76	Wm. Thomas *	May/73		x	8	810	113
6/10/76	Robert Browne	June/75	wife	x	6	770	114
6/17/76	Evan Jones	March/72	wife		1	70	114
11/10/76	Jane Rixam	1676	daughter	x	2	340	118
1/13/77	Thomas Stanyan	May/75	wife; 5 children	x	4	950	122
1/30/77	Thomas Turpin			x	1	170	124
1/ 1/77	Robert Gough		wife	x	2	400	148
11/30/78	ffrancis Boult Gent.		wife, slaves, and servants	x		600	190

* Illegal grant

[16]

Scrutiny of the above tables discloses several instances (note asterisks) of illegal grants. Thomas and James Smith received 200 acres under a grant of May 21, 1672, and a like amount on April 12, 1675: in both instances for two servants brought over in August 1671. Lieutenant Colonel Godfrey seems to have counted himself as one of the members of the groups for which he laid claim. So prevalent did this sort of abuse become that very definite instructions were sent out to Governor Moreton in 1682 describing the procedure to be followed in the granting of land by patent.

> Any person haveing transported himself & servants into that part of Carolina that is under your Governmt. to plant shall make it appear to your selfe and the Grand Councell by pro-duceing his servants before them or by Certificate upon Oath and his or her owne name & his servants name being Recorded in the books of the grand Councell he haveing Subscribed as is in these our Instructions before mentioned you are thereupon to Issue out a warrant to the Surveyor generall to lay him out a parcell of land according to the proportions & Rules directed in these our Instructions & ye Surveyor Generalls Retourne thereupon being Recorded you are to pass the following grant for the qt of land due which is to be affixed to ye plott of his Land.[25]

The instructions then set forth the form of the patent to be used in these words:

> William Earle of Craven one of the Lords of His Majesties Most honble privey Councell Ld. Liftenant of the County of Middlesex & Borrough of Soathwarke Pallatine & ye rest of the true & absolute Lords and proprietors of Carolina to all to whome these psents shall come greating in our Lord God ever lasting. Know ye that we ye Sd. Lords Proprietors according to our Instructions Dated Whitehall the 10th day of May 1682 Remaineing upon in our province of Carolina doe hereby grant _____ of the said province aforesaid Planter a plantation lyeing & being in the County of _____ bounded _____. The said Lands being due to the said _____ by and for the trans-portation of _____ persons whose names are upon Record under this patent to have and to hold the said plantation unto ye said _____ his heairs and assignes for ever with prviledge of hawking, hunding, fishing & fowleing within the bounds of ye same with all wood and trees wth what else there is thereon growing Standing or being Except all mines, mineralls, gemms or pretious Stones yealding & paying therefore unto us our heirs & successors yearley one penny of Lawful money of

England for every of the said Akers to be holden of us in free & common Soccage; the first payment of the Rent to begin the twenty ninth day of September in the yeare of our Lord _____. Given at Charles Towne in Berkly County in ye province of Carolina aforesaid under the great seale appointed for that purpose this _____ day of _____ in the yeare of our Lord _____.[26]

Copies of warrants were to be sent to the Lords Proprietors every three months.

These precautions were still not sufficient to prevent illegal grants, for in 1686 additional instructions were sent to Governor Moreton: "If we find this humour (objection to signing a contract with them) persisted in, we shall withdraw our power for granting lands for servants brought thighter. —We are informed that divers persons have gotten possession of vast quantities of land, greater than are due to them for the servants they have imported—. Before you pass grants of land to any of these persons, you will strictly examine what right they have thereto, and let none have land but according to our instructions." [27]

This strict oversight and the deeding of land only to such as should have proved themselves entitled to it may have reduced the number of invalid grants, but it also put a damper on the business of importing servants. There would be no difficulty for the settler entitled to land on his own account, but the speculators evidently considered their profits too small under the more rigid system. Two years later, it was reported that "the change of land grants by patents to grants by indenture has driven away people from the colony and kept many more from coming to it." [28]

According to the Lords Proprietors' Instructions of February 6, 1693, grants were to be made to such as come "to plant and inhabit in Carolina *and are content to Signe the counterpart of the Deed according to the forms hereunto annexed.*" This was the point of differentiation from the earlier grant by patent; now the grantee was a signatory to the indenture for land. In accordance with this plan, Henry Bayley, with a warrant dated August 15, 1694, was "obliged within 90 days from ye date of said warrt. to signe the Counterpart of ye Indented Deed, for paying the Lords Rent &c." [29] By further instructions of July 26, 1700, when warrants were made out in favor of those importing other persons, the Register and Secretary of the Colony was "to marke ye Names of those in ye

Register of persons imported for whom it is granted with a Cross that it may appear land is already granted for them thereby ye granting land twice for ye Same persons be Avoyded." [30]

The attempt to stop the abuses in the head-right system blocked the chances for profit in bringing servants. Therefore it was necessary to grant bounties on the importation of servants. In 1698 an act was passed which provided a bounty for encouraging the importation of white servants. The only objection which seems to have been raised was that voiced by the Solicitor General to the Council of Trade and Plantations: "As to the Act for promoting the importation of servants, Nov. 3, 1698, Mr. Attorney General and myself reported upon a similar Act from Montserratt, 1696, that we were doubtful how far it might encourage kidnapping or stealing white servants, but I am informed by Mr. Cary, who then appeared as Agent for Montserratt, and now appears as agent for Antigua, that that objection did not weigh anything with your Lordships." [31] This reflected the general attitude of the home authorities, and is contemporaneous with the passage by the Carolina legislature of "An Act for the Encouragement of the Importation of White Servants." [32] A similar act was ratified on June 30, 1716. [33] Thus the initiative for encouraging servant importation was taken over by the colonial legislature.

Under this system the Proprietors granted land: first, to freemen who would immigrate; second, to those who would bring in others (including servants and slaves); third, to servants for their own account after they had served their time. The first group does not touch immediately upon the servant question. The following documents illustrate fulfillment of the provisions for a grant under the second group:

> Mr. John Barksdale had a Warrtt: out of the Secrtys office Dated the 7th day of June 1695. Signed by the Honoble: Joseph Blake Esqr. Landgrave & Governr for six hundred & sixtie Acres of Land. on Accott of Arraivell Rights. of Ten Psons viz: Mr. John Barksdale, Mrs. Sarah Barksdale: his wife, Charles: Thomas: John and Mary Barksdale their Children, and oliver. ffrancis and Eliz ffrancis: Else Allery & Mary ffalkoner Jno: Edwards: Servants Gay: Maria and Betty: Slaves all which said Psons. were Imported into this Pvince of Carolina on the propper. Cost & Charge of the Said Barksdale—. [34]

The next document was an example of warrants to servants out of their time:

Carolina   By ye Honoble—the Governr—Henry. Bayley: had a Warrant out of ye Secrtys office, dated ye 15th Augst: 1694. Signed by the Honoble. Tho: Smith Esqr, Landgrave & Governr for one hundred Acres of Land on ye Accott of arraivell Rights. due for himselfe & Sarah his wife, which were Imported into this part of ye Pvince of Carolina in ye year 168___ servants to Sr. Richard Carle. and Mr. Thomas Ferguson to Setle here, The said Henry Bayley is obliged within 90 days from ye Date of said wrrtt: to signe the Counterpart of ye Indented Deed, for paying the Lords Rent (& etc.) . . .[35]

The system of family rights was continued beyond the Proprietary period. In 1731 the government bounty for servants whose time was out was as follows: "His Majesty . . . grants to every European Servant, whether Man or Woman, 50 Acres of Land free of all Rents for 10 Years, which shall be distributed to them after having served their Master for the Time agreed on." [36] The rents referred to were the quitrents. This system lasted until the Revolution.

CHAPTER II

White Servants Meet the Labor Demand

THE SECOND AND REALLY PRINCIPAL reason for the importation of white servants is to be found in the demands of the labor market. The list of servants from Barbados is typical of any such group arriving in the early days. There were two sawyers, one carpenter, one tailor, two planters, one woman servant, and three without special designations.[1] Such a distribution of skills might well have been the best possible selection to meet the needs of an infant colony.

As already noted, even Virginia, a colony of many years standing, had not in 1670 become convinced of the superiority of Negroes as field hands. Both white servants and Negro slaves were brought into the colony from the beginning. Later, when rice began to dominate as the great staple crop, the question was settled in favor of the cheaper and hardier labor. But rice did not monopolize the attention of the planters until the 1730's. Even after this period there was an opportunity for white field labor in the development of indigo, which was introduced in the 1740's. "Patricola" in 1747 actually urged greater interest in the planting of indigo for this very reason. This crop, "Patricola" wrote, "can bear the Charge of a long Land-Carriage as well as Deer skins, and may be carried on with a great deal of Ease by white People only, without Blacks, which Rice cannot be, [therefore] it could not but invite Numbers of new Settlers amongst us, and greatly tend to the peopling and strengthening our Western Frontiers"[2]. . . . It was only on the eve of the Revolution, during the last great colonial period of prosperity (1770-1773), that the economy matured and the need for field labor was met entirely, at least on the coast, by Negroes. It took one hundred years for such specialization to develop. (See Appendix III.) Meanwhile white indentured servants were continuously in demand although always in declining numbers.

As the colony developed there came about a division of labor, with the Negro slaves doing the field work and the white indentured servants working as mechanics or artisans in the town and as clerical workers and overseers on the plantations. Thomas Lynch, the master of three plantations, Hopsewee, Indian Bluff, and Pleasant Meadow, obviously ran his estates by using this division of labor, as his will filed in the records of the Probate Court proves. The total value of Lynch's estate was £55,958/9/3. There were 160 Negro slaves valued at £60 to £500 each. There were also the following white servants mentioned in the estate valuation:

1 Servant Alex. Agnen and wife for one years Serv. £50
1 Boy, James McDonal, for 5 years 50
1 Gilbert Guthries, for 3½ years 35
1 David Guthries, for 2½ years 40
1 Robert Jones, 2½ years . . . . 40 [3]

Especially in demand were those experienced in various trades. Many advertisements of servants imported and offered for sale specified some distinguishing mark of fitness for service. John and Edmond Atkin advertised "The Service of a great Number of German Swiss People just arrived in the Ship *Eagle, Wm. Walker* Master from *Holland,* . . . for a Term of 1 and a half, 2 or 3 Years, in Proportion to the Value demanded, which will be only *Six* Pistoles, or *Thirty Six* Pounds *per* head of any age above 14 Years, excepting for any Man who is a Tradesman. There are amongst them (some single but most with Families greater or less) several Carpenters, Butchers, Weavers, Smiths, (one of which undertakes to perform almost anything to be wrought in Iron) Shoemakers, Taylors, one Cooper and one Sadler, the rest (being the Major part) are Husbandmen." [4] Runaway notices, appearing in almost every issue of the *Gazette,* generally stated the servant's trade as a mark of identification. In the list of such, practically every field was covered: from valets [5] and fencing-masters [6] to bricklayers [7] and carpenters; [8] from gardeners [9] and farm-hands [10] to shoemakers [11] and tailors.[12]

Benjamin Whitaker advised the public that: "Whereas I have purchased a Servant who is a Chimney-sweeper, intending thereby to prevent the Danger that doth threaten this Town, by Chimneys often catching Fire, which may be the Ruin thereof; and many complaints have been made to me by the Inhabitants, that the Chimney-sweeper doth neglect to sweep their Chimneys, tho' being by them required; Therefore to prevent Complaints, I do give Notice to all Persons, that they may agree by the Year, to have their Chimneys sweep'd every Month, or oftener if required, according

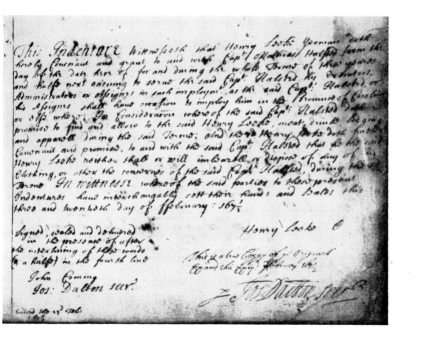

Indentures of white servants were copied in the *Records of the Register and Secretary of the Province*, now in the South Carolina Archives. These two, dated 1669 and 1671/2, were among the first recorded.

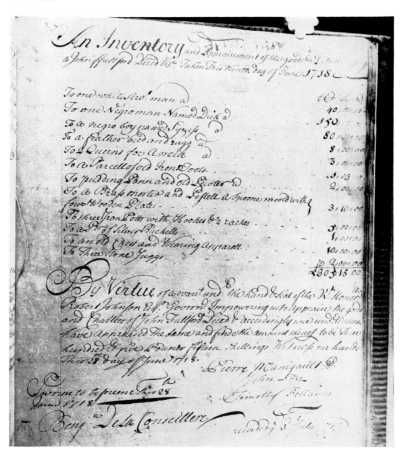

Above, another early indenture, dated 1673/4. The inventory (below) is proof positive that there were white servants in South Carolina in 1718.

to the Number of Funnels, at reasonable Rates to be paid Quarterly, so long as the said Chimney-sweeper continues in Health, and is a Servant to *Daniel Greene.*" [13]

TABLE III

Trades of Servants, as Noted in Gazette Advertisements

BAKER: George Michael Woller "claims to be a Butcher and Baker, but works best at the plow." . . . . June 5th and 12th, 1755

BARBER: Philip Jones . . . . Nov., 4th, 11th and 18th, 1732
Nathaniel Peters . . . . . . April 23d and 30th, May 7th, 1741

BARKEEPER: Richard Aalder . . . . April 9th and 23rd, 1773

BLACKSMITH: John Willis . . . . June 5th, 14th and 21st, 1742
Robert Cunningham—
February 7th, 14th and 21st, 1736
Christopher Chezus—
Jan. 22nd, 29th and Feb., 5th, 1750

BRICKLAYER: William Dick . May 14th and 28th and June 4th, 1772
Richard Dearsley . . . . Oct. 12th and 19th, 1734
Thomas Cawood . . . . Oct. 12th and 19th, 1734
James Powell . . . . June 16th, 23rd and 30th, 1739

BUTCHER: John Frederick Herter . . . . Jan. 29th and Feb. 5th, 1750
Henry Hertel . . . . Jan. 29th and Feb. 5th, 1750
John Daniel Hertel . . . . Jan. 29th and Feb. 5th, 1750
Charles Turner . . . . Nov. 12th, 19th, 26th, 1750
Henry Grotte . . . . Jan. 11th, 1768

CABINET MAKER: Esparee Lamare . . . . Sept. 10th, 17th, 24th, 1753

CARPENTER: John Peter Bovet . Dec. 23d and 30th and Jan. 6th, 1733
William Merick . . . . April 14th, 21st, 1734
George Lesley . . . . Jan. 19th and 26th, 1738
Abraham Daphne—
June 18th and 25th and July 2nd, 1753
Gasper Morgendaler. . . . April 9th, 16th and 23rd, 1737
Marmaduke Tiley . . . . Sept. 3rd, 1737
John Brooks . . . . Feb. 26th, March 5th and 12th, 1741
John Hughs . . . . July 30th, Aug. 6th and 15th, 1741
Robert Allen . . . . Aug. 16th, 23rd and 30th, 1742
Timothy Grover . . . . Dec. 8th, 15th and 22nd, 1758

TABLE III—*Continued*

JOYNER: Gasper Gerber ....April 23rd and 30th, 1750
    Robert Clason ....February 27th and Mch. 6th, 1755
BOAT BUILDER: Thomas Bill—
                   Mch. 12th, 19th, 26th and Apr. 2nd, 1744
SHIP CARPENTER: Israel Cowin ....June 17th, 1745
    Paul Christian Wolf—
                 April 15th, 22nd, 29th, 1751
CHIMNEY SWEEP: ....Jan. 20th and 27th and Feb. 4, 1733
COLLECTOR: Thomas Bond .March 30th and Apr. 6th and 13th, 1734
    James Craddock ....Jan. 1st and 15th, 1737
COOPER: Peter Robertson ....Jan. 6th, 13th and 20th, 1733
    George Dempster .. June 29th and July 6th and 13th, 1734
    Thomas Moore ....Feb. 9th, 16th and 23rd, 1738
FARMER: Samuel Chandler ....Dec. 8th, 15th and 22nd, 1758
    Peter Dantzler ....Jan. 29th, and Feb. 5th, 1750
FARM-HAND: John Procey .. May 28th and June 4th and 25th, 1750
PLANTER: Evan Howell ...Rec. Sec'y of Province—Dec. 23rd, 1670
    John Cole ....Rec. Sec'y of Province—Dec. 23rd, 1670
FENCING MASTER: Thomas Butler—
                 July 20th, 27th and Aug. 3rd, 1734
FILE CUTTER: William Clews—
                 May 18th and 25th and June 1st, 1734
GARDENER: Thomas Field ....June 22nd and 29th, 1734
    James Cupit ....Feb. 12th, 19th and 26th, 1737
    Peter Broderick .....Oct. 1st, 8th, 15th and 22nd, 1744
    Robert Bard ....Jan. 8th, 15th and 22nd, 1750
MASON: Tho. Stranghan ....March 12th, 19th and 26th, 1744
MILLER: Yerick Groener ....Jan. 23rd and 30th and Feb. 6th, 1755
NAIL MAKER: Joseph Fillow ......March 3rd, 10th and 17th, 1746
NAILOR: Peter Laurens ....Feb. 7th, 14th and 21st, 1736
PAINTER: Walter Wallace ....April 5th, 1735
PERUKE MAKER: John Carroll—
                 May 16th and 25th and June 1st, 1748
    Patrick Welsh—
                 Aug. 6th and 13th and 20th, 1737
PRINTER: Robert Whitaker ....July and Sept., 1751
ROPE MAKER: Rich. Ashton ......July 16th, 23rd and 30th, 1737
SADLER: Barthol Topler ....April 9th, 16th and 23rd, 1737

TABLE III—*Continued*

SAILOR: Benjamin Chase ....Nov. 13th, 20th and 27th, 1736
John West ....April 30th and May 7th and 14th, 1737
PATROON OF PILOT BOAT: Ja. Mathews—
June 29th and July 6th and 13th, 1738
Alexander Crombie—
Nov. 13th, 20th and 27th, 1736
PETTIAUGER MAN: John Casper Faust—
Dec. 18th and 24th, Jan. 1st, 15th, 22nd and 29th, 1737
John Matthews—
April 28th, May 5th and 12th, 1733
Francis Burn ....Feb. 9th and 16th, 1734
Samuel Ward ....Feb. 2nd, 9th and 16th, 1734
SAWYER: Richard Poore—Rec. Sec'y of Province ..Dec. 30th, 1670
Thomas Witty—Rec. Sec'y of Province ..Dec. 23rd, 1670
Charles Gastril ....June 16th, 23rd and 30th, 1739
CARPENTER: Thomas Patterson—Rec. Sec'y of Province—
Dec. 23rd, 1670
SCRIVENER: John Brooks—Cal. St. Pap. Col., xvii, 326—
May 1st, 1699
TEACHER: James Hewitt ....Aug. 4th, 11th and 18th, 1733
(Scholar): Richard Lee ....July 13th, 20th and 27th, 1734
(Student): Hugh Forbess ...June 29th and July 6th and 13th, 1734
SHOEMAKER: Hugh Newtone ......May 31st and June 7th, 1740
Paul Traut ....Jan. 8th and 15th, 1754
William Welsh ....June 10th and 17th, 1732
Rich. Tilly ....Aug. 21st and Oct. 2nd and 9th, 1736
John Paul Traut ....Jan. 8th and 15th, 1754
Hans Adam Guder—
Sept. 30th and Oct. 7th and 14th, 1745
John Daniel ....Sept. 10th, 17th and 24th, 1753
Samuel Wright—
Aug. 17th and 24th and Sept. 1st, 1752
William Madame—
Aug. 17th and 24th and Sept. 1st, 1752
(Cobbler): Richard Acton ...Oct. 18th and 25th and Nov. 1st, 1742
STONE CUTTER: John Saxon ....Sept. 30th, 1732
BARBER-SURGEON: David Ludowick Thomas—
Jan. 23rd and 30th and Feb. 6th, 1755

TABLE III—*Continued*

SURGEON : —paid for by the Assembly—
(J.C.H.A., No. 5., p. 182)—November, 1716
TAYLOR : Samuel Buzard—Rec. Sec'y of Province . . Dec. 23rd, 1670
Caleb Lowle . . . . Feb. 19th and 26th and March 4th, 1732
Jenkin James . . . . June 16th, 23rd and 30th, 1739
John Thompson . . . . Nov. 16th, 23rd and 30th, 1734
Walter Martin . . . . April 23rd and 30th and May 7th, 1741
Samuel Hall . . . . July 9th, 16th and 23rd, 1744
Joseph Waters . . . . Sept. 10th, 17th and 24th, 1744
Christian Findling . . . . Jan. 15th, 22nd and 29th, 1753
Henry Lawson . . . . March 1st and 8th, 1760
WEAVER : Francis Lewis Perry . . April 23rd and 30th and 7th, 1750
John Millar . . . . Jan. 11th, 1768
John Soman . . . . Jan. 11th, 1768
WHEELWRIGHT : Conrade Minky . . . . May 20th and 27th, 1751

Johannes Henric Bokker. . June 5th and 12th, 1755
While the above does not purport to be a perfect record, it roughly comprises the majority of trades practiced. It certainly is illustrative of the large field covered by white servants. Moreover, since these items are taken from the records, just as they happen to occur, the list fairly represents the probable relative demand for skilled workmen of different sorts. Charleston evidently believed in being well dressed. There were nineteen shoemakers and nine tailors. The carpenters were also nine in number.

In 1763, Henry Laurens wrote Captain Thomas Courtin: "I shall be much obliged to you to procure for me on terms of three years a sober steady Man, a Cooper that is a good hand at his business, provided he will come out for £25 Stg. per Annum & his board & diet; his passage to be paid by me but deducted out of his Wages, which I may abate if he behaves well." [14] This letter suggests the difficulty of getting such a man as was needed in the regular course of importing indentured servants. The supply was by this time falling off and, furthermore, paid labor was, in general, beginning to supplant the earlier system.

CHAPTER III

White Servants as a Measure of Defense

THE THIRD REASON FOR IMPORTING servants was for protection. The Spanish in Florida looked upon the constant southerly extension of English settlements in the late seventeenth century with as jealous an eye as they had viewed the French attempts of a century earlier. While actual hostilities did not break out until the opening of the eighteenth century, the loss of runaway servants and Negroes, rivalry in the Indian trade, and the unsettled state of affairs in their respective mother-countries all contributed to the suspicion with which the Carolina and Florida settlements regarded each other. Moreover, danger was always to be apprehended from the Indians, whether incited by Spanish intrigue or not.

Considerable effort was put forth for a time to maintain friendly relations with the neighboring tribes. In June 1682 the Lords Proprietors were forced to "forbid any person to take up land within two miles, on the same side of a river, of an Indian settlement." Those who did take up lands near Indian settlements were to help the Indians "fence their corn that no damage be done by the hogs and cattle of the English." [1] The Lords Proprietors considered the Anglo-Indian society as a whole, but by 1690 the major power in the colony had passed into the hands of a group of merchants who were primarily interested in commercial profits to be earned in the fur and skin trade. Thus, the question of Indian relations became of paramount importance and the occasions for friction greatly increased.

The administrations of Governors Archdale and Blake were generally peaceful and prosperous; but the latter's successor, James Moore, who came to office in 1700, adopted an aggressive policy toward both the Spaniards and the Indians. The rupture between England and Spain led to an invasion of Florida from Carolina. The governor was unsuccessful in this, but followed the campaign with a more successful war against the Indians. In 1712-1717 two

Indian wars were fought: with the Tuscaroras and with the Yamassees. While the issue was usually favorable to the colonists, this chronic situation on the border represented a constant danger.

The colony was so desirous of having settlers on the frontier that it even went into the importing business. A message from the Upper to the Lower House on February 18, 1700, indicated that the Receiver had had for some time on his hands the white servants "which came in Capt. flaville." It was urged that they be disposed of as soon as possible so that their services could be made use of and the government be reimbursed for the expense of importing them.[2] This is certainly suggestive of public ownership.

The act of June 7, 1712, was designed to foster importation of servants either directly or indirectly by the support of the colonial government. The first article of the act empowered the "publick Receiver for the time being . . . dureing the Term of *Four* Years, after the Ratification of this Act, [to] pay out of the publick Treasury of this Province, the Sum of *Fourteen* Pounds Current Money to the Owners or Importers of each healthy Male British Servant, betwixt the Age of *Twelve* and *Thirty* Years, as soon as the Said Servant or Servants are assigned over into his Hands by him or them to whom they belong." The second article authorized the Public Receiver to dispose of these servants to the inhabitants of the Province "as much to the publick Advantage as he can, either for Money paid in Hand, or for Bonds payable in *Four* Months," and drawing interest at ten per cent thereafter. Article four provided that "in Case it so happen that there remains on any Occasions some Servants, whom the Receiver can neither dispose of in any reasonable time, nor employ to the Benefit of the Publick, he shall with the Approbation of Mr. *William Gibbon,* Mr. *Andrew Allen* and Mr. *Benjamin Godin,* or any two of them, sett these Servants Free, taking their own Bonds, or as good Security as he can get, for the Payment of the Sum or Sums of Money, as the Publick has expended in their behalf. . . ." The sixth article prohibited the importation of any who "were ever in any Prison or Gaol, or publickly stigmatized for any Matter criminal by the Laws of *Great Britain.*"[3]

It was felt that those who had had experience fighting in European wars would make good settlers on the American frontier. It did not make any difference which side they had fought on in Europe, for in America all Europeans would probably stand together against the marauding Indians. The most exposed colonies were therefore looked upon as the most suitable dumping ground for the disbanded soldiery of the mother country.[4]

After the suppression of the 1715 rebellion it was decided to send some of the rebels to America. On May 10, 1716, the Lords Proprietors advised Governor Craven: "We having received two Letters from Mr. Secretary Stanhope signifying his Majtys pleasure in relation to such of the Rebels who were taken at Preston and are to be transported to his plantations in America that as soon as any of the Rebels shall land in any port of our province of Carolina you shall appoint a sufficient Guard for securing them till they are dispos'd of according to the Terms of the Indentures they have enter'd into here and such of the Rebels who have not enter'd into Indentures here you are to offer to them that they enter into the like Indentures with the others, Vizt. to serve for the space of seven years and in case of their refusal to enter into such Indentures you are to give proper certificates to those that purchase them that it is his Majesty's pleasure that they shall continue servants to them & their assigns for the term of seven Years, which certificates you are to cause to be recorded for the satisfaction of those who purchase them, lest they should attempt to make their Escape not being bound. We do hereby strictly require & command you to Obey these orders in every particular. . . ."[5]

Some of these rebels were actually bought by the government. On August 1, 1716, Deputy Governor Robert Daniell sent a message to the Commons House of Assembly, explaining that the danger from Indian attacks was so imminent that he had taken it upon himself to purchase "thirty of the Highland Scots rebels at thirty Pounds per head to be paid for in fifteen days; and . . . [he adds that he] . . . would have contracted for the whole number, but that I could not persuade the commissioners that they had powers enough."[6] On the fourth an "act to Impower the Commissioners appointed to Stamp Fifteen Thousand Pounds in Bills of Credit to Pay for Thirty Two White Servants Purchased by the Honourable the Governor" was ratified.[7] But public ownership did not become a practice, for the places where such servants could be used were limited. A few proposals were made in later years but they were not acted upon. In 1726 a committee of the Assembly reported: it is their opinion that "it will greatly reduce the charge for manning the said Forts if five servants be purchased for each and in order to procure the same we propose that Captain Stewart or some other person be treated with to transport such a number which we believe may be agreed for at £ 40 or £ 50 per head indented for four years." [8] Again, in January 1741, Lieutenant Governor Bull suggested the plan of purchasing sufficient single men to man the forts.[9]

The public policy was actually to hire servants as they were needed. As privately owned servants were liable to service in the militia and patrols, absence of public ownership does not militate against the theory that servants were used in the defense of the colony.

The servants were really more important as a defense against possible slave insurrections than as a defense against the enemy from without. The importation of slaves was a matter of individual initiative. As the culture of rice increased, the demand for slaves grew. More and more they furnished the bulk of agricultural labor. However, the very growth in number of slaves created a new demand for servants.

Protection against a Negro insurrection was secured in two ways: first, by limitations and restrictions especially designed to prevent slaves from congregating; second, by providing a proportion of white men sufficient to defeat conspiracies or outbreaks. Bills "for the better security of the Inhabitants of this Province against the insurrections and other wicked attempts of negroes and other Slaves" [10] alternate with those "for the better securing this Province from Negro insurrections & encouraging of poor people by employing them in Plantations." [11] In 1711 Governor Gibbes asked the House of Assembly to "consider the legal quantities of negroes that are daily brought into this Governt., and the small number of whites that comes amongst us, and how many are lately dead, or gone off. How insolent and mischievous the negroes are become, and to consider the Negro Act doth not reach up to some of the crimes they have lately been guilty of." As a remedy, he suggested the importation of whites at the public charge.[12] This was not done, but a law was passed in 1712 to force plantation owners to take servants. No person after the ratification of the 1712 act "Shall Settle or manage any Plantation, Cowpen or Stock that Shall be Six Miles distant from his usual Place of abode and where in Six Negroes or

Slaves Shall be Imployed without One or more White Person Liveing and Resideing upon the Same Plantation, upon Penalty or Forfeiture of Forty Shillings for each Month so Offending." [13]

Very real efforts were put forward at this period to encourage importation of servants. A large part of the debates in both Council and House centered upon plans for maintaining a safe equilibrium of population. In June 1716 it was recommended "that all persons that have a plantation and ten working hands and no white man but the master shall be put into the lot [that is, provided from the first supply of whites imported], so that every one in the country May 1st have one white servant . . . every one that hath twenty negroes, to come into the second lot . . . every one that hath thirty to come in the third lot; &c." [14] As further encouragement, it was suggested that a money "bounty be given of five pounds per head to every master who shall import white servants." [15] The first comprehensive act dealing specifically with the white servant question was then passed in 1717.[16]

In June 1722 a series of questions was put to ascertain the sentiment of the House on various details of this subject. It was voted that the master should *not* be deemed or accounted for one "white person, in meeting the requirement that there be such on each plantation." It was voted that Negroes and not lands should be "taxable toward the encouragement of bringing over white persons." [17] In April 1725 the committee appointed to consider the best method "for bringing white Servants into this Province" recommended "First that every person possessing ten Negroes or other taxable Slaves be obliged to hire one white Servant Man or boy of a proper age to be & Reside upon the Plantation or Trackt of Land where such Negroes or slaves are employed & so in proportion to a large large Number so possesst." The third point provided "That all persons who shall neglect or refuse to purchase or provide such white Servants as aforesaid be liable to such a Penalty as this house shall think fitt to be appropriated to bearing the Charges of Importing such Servants as aforesaid." [18] In 1726 this provision demanded a regular ratio of one white man to every ten slaves; [19] and in the following year, "for every ten male Slaves— from the Age of Sixteen to Sixty." [20] Toward the close of 1739, in addition to the required white for every ten slaves, there had to be one white man supplied by every owner of 4,000 acres; an additional white for each 2,000 acres over that amount, and up to 20,000 acres; and from that amount up, one for each 1,000 acres.[21]

In September 1740 the eighth of a set of resolutions submitted by the House to the Council argues, "The Preamble to the sd Act declares as a reason for passing the same that the best way to prevent fatal Mischiefs for the future from Insurrections of our Negroes would be to Establish a Method by which the Importation of Negroes should be made a necessary Means of introducing a proportionable number of white Inhabts. . . ." [22]

It was not sufficient merely to require one white man for every so many acres of land. A very necessary part of the machinery of control was the patrol. This duty was performed by those liable to service in the militia, and was under the supervision of regular militia officers who were made responsible for their respective districts. Frequent provision was made for the service of privately owned servants, both in the militia and on military expeditions beyond the borders. On June 30, 1716, was ratified "An Act for the better Setling and Regulating the Militia." Section seven provided "that every Master, Mistriss or other Person that at any time hath the Command of any Servant, Shall at his or their Costs and Charges Provide and furnish each man with all and every Particular of the Armes, ammunition and Accoutrements aforesaid, and the Said man Servant So Provided Shall be Sent to the Place of Rendezvous at Such time and times as Shall be appointed as aforesaid under the Pains and Penalties of fifty Shillings for each Day (of neglect)." It is further provided that if the fault be the servant's, he "Shall receive such Moderate Corporal Punishment as the Head of the Said Company (the master having made proof before its commissioned officers), by Order of the Chief Commission Officer then Present as he Shall think fit." [23]

In 1727 the Committee of the House recommended "That the Patroles be on the same Establishment as by the Militia Law is Directed and that all white Servants be lyable to all Private Musters, and other Duties as the rest of the Militia are." [24] In May 1740 it had been agreed, among other amendments to the Patrol Bill, that "The Clause concerning white Servants [is] to be struck out both in the Title and Body of the Bill." [25] While this contains the suggestion that white servants were no longer to be used, it is more likely that what was struck out was the requirement that servants furnish their own equipment. In December 1741 the House committee appointed to revise the Patrol Act reported £25,500 as the necessary budget to be provided.[26] Two districts for each of the thirty-seven companies ("exclusive of Charles Town") and a separate district organization for the "Town Neck" gave seventy-five units of patrol jurisdiction. The commander of each district was to receive £100 per annum and each of four patrolmen £60. Section four of the Act contained the requirement of "finding" a "white man well provided, with a horse and accoutrements, to do patrol duty when required (that is) for the two months that they shall be appointed." [27] In February 1745 every plantation having slaves had to furnish at least one such man; for every fifty slaves, two; and one additional man for every twenty-five slaves in excess of fifty.[28] In the Act of 1746 there was a "white servants excepted" clause which had the latter significance. This latter Act provided "that the masters of all overseers and white *white* [white repeated; but evidently the intent is "white servants", for the marginal summary opposite this paragraph reads "Masters to accoutre their servants"], who by this act are obliged to do patrol service, shall be obliged to furnish their overseers and servants with a horse and furniture for such service." [29]

The Charles Town watch exercised the duties of a patrol in the one urban center of South Carolina. In 1725 numerous complaints were made of the inefficiency of this amateur body; to which it was answered "it cannot be expected that the persons of whom the present Watch consists who being chiefly servants and apprentices cannot serve the Publick by night and their masters by day." [30]

Evidence of the actual performance of military service by white servants appears in petitions to the Assembly praying payment for such services rendered. On May 2, 1716, the petition of John Lane (or Law) was read "relating to his white servant killed in the war." [31] On the eleventh, the House was of the opinion that an allowance should be made. Objection to the use of white servants in the militia seemed to arise rather from fear of losing the servant than from lack of trust as to the performance of his duty. In June 1717 a controversy arose between the Governor and Council and the House over the use of servants in the ranger service. The lower house contended for the exception of "white servants"; but finally agreed for "the words (white servants excepted) [to] be rased out of the said Bill on condition that there be inserted a clause to make satisfaction to the master or mistress of said servant, in case they be killed in the Public service." [32]

Actual military service was not the only public function performed by servants. In 1717 payment was ordered of "the sume of one hundred and sixty Pounds . . . to Robert Gilcrest for his own and his man's service to the Public in his late Journey to and from the Cherikees." [33] In November 1734, "His Excellency Signd an Order Directed to Alexr. Parris Esqr., Publick Treasurer to pay to Jeremiah Taylor what is due to him and two Servants pressed to Convey Sevl. Passengers designed to people Purysburgh, . . ." [34] Again, in 1736, Mrs. Russell asked payment for the time of a white servant whom her husband had been obliged to buy. Major Russell had been agent to the Cherokees and the clerk appointed to assist him had failed to appear. The House voted Mrs. Russell, now a widow, 40 shillings per diem for the eleven days public service for the clerk.[35] William Carwithin petitioned for payment because his servant was impressed "in the late alarm—to work as a carpenter in the service of the Government." [36] William Fitzpatrick wanted to be paid for two servants taken to Georgia and enlisted under Oglethorpe.[37] Presumably, the two men for whose services wages for one month to the amount of £24 were paid to Thomas Ladson on October 20, 1728, were white servants. The wages were paid "for Look Outs at the mouth of North Edisto" and slaves would scarcely have been chosen for such important and responsible work.[38]

The most serious threat of a slave insurrection which appears in the records of the assembly was in 1733, when the House apprised the governor of information received concerning several large gatherings of Negroes, from which serious danger might result. One of these meetings, as investigation showed, had been attended by some three hundred slaves. The message recommended the arrest and close confinement of ten slaves, who were named as leaders, and the ordering of the militia companies to be prepared to march "at an hour's warning if there be occasion." [39]

But two years later, "the Humble Remonstrance of your Majesty's Governor, Council and Assembly of your Majesty's Province of South Carolina" voiced complaint of another danger. "The Importation of Negroes we crave leave to Inform your Majty. is a Species of Trade, that has exceedingly increasd of late in this Province where many Negroes are now Train'd up to be Handycraft Tradesmen;

to the great Discouragement of your Majesty's white Subjects who come here to Setle with a view of Employement in their several Occupations but must often give way to a People in Slavery, which we daily discover to be a great Obstruction to the Settlement of this Frontier with white People." [40]

It was agreed in the House on April 1, 1743, "that no slaves that shall hereafter be brought up to any mechanic trades shall be suffered to be hired out or to work for any other than their own masters." [41] The House Committee on Charles Town recommended on February 2, 1750, "That no Handicrafts Man shall hereafter teach a Negro his Trade in the said Town belonging to any Person but himself on any pretence whatsoever." [42] Negroes, however, rapidly came into use as mechanics on the plantations. Within a few years after date of the above recommendations, the "Inventory of Hugh Cartwright" showed four lots of slaves, aggregating fifty-five males and thirty-seven females—all valued at £16,774. The highest individual values, except for tradesmen, were £280 for Daniel, a field hand, and £250 for Tom, a Negro overseer. With one exception, these are lower than any of those practicing trades, a list of whom follows:

Cyrus, a Bricklayer £350
Smart, a Bricklayer 400
Simon, a Tanner and Currier 300
Jack, a Blacksmith 300
Robin, a Corker 400
Boston, a Sawyer (and his wife and two children) 700
Toney, a Sawyer (and others) 550
Prince, a Brickmaker (and others) 650
York, a Carpenter 500
Little Carolina, Sailmaker 300
Quamina, a Blacksmith 400
Corporation, a Butcher 300
Greenwich, a Brickmaker 200
George, a Boatman 323
Scipio, a Boatman 415
Tartar, a Boatman 316
Carolina, a Shoemaker 456
Jacob, a Sawyer .... 408 [43]

There were other reasons for shutting down on the importation of slaves. A writer in the *Gazette* of March 9th, 1738, argued that "*Negroes* may be said to be the Bait proper for catching a *Carolina* Planter, as certain as Beef to catch a Shark. How many under the Notion of 18 Months Credit, have been tempted to buy more Negroes than they could possibly expect to pay [for] in 3 Years!" After advising that each planter figure out his exact chances (he, himself, estimating that a man may be safe in increasing his slaves ten per cent per annum), the writer concluded, "Were it possible to prevent any Negroes to be imported for 3 Years to come, I am perswaded it would be for the general Advantage of all the Inhabitants in this Province, and the only Means to relieve us from the Load of Debts we are now owing to Great Britain, which I believe is equal to the Amount of 3 Years Produce." [44] This has much the sound of the stock argument in favor of letting the United States catch up with its foreign-labor supply; but it was prophetic at least of the prodigality of management which was to prove so vital a weakness in the agricultural system of the South. There were many other opponents of unrestricted slave importation.

In February 1750 the report of the committee in charge of the general security, health, and convenience of the inhabitants of Charleston recommended that, in view of the excessive number of slaves, "some Proper Restraint may be put to this growing Evil, to reduce the present number, And that all due encouragement may be given to white Inhabitants to reside in the said Town, it is proposed that all white Persons who will accept of any servile Labour, such as Porter &c, shall have the preference to all Jobs that offer, and be intitled to an additional Hire per Diem. . . ." [45]

In the light of the above, the Acadians should have been welcomed to South Carolina in the 1750's. They were not, however, for they were looked upon as a "fifth column"—French Catholics who might stir up the Indians and slaves.

In June 1756 Governor Lyttlelton reported "that the whole number landed here was 1,023, of whom 109 have died and 273 have been shipped off or made their escape." [46] Some had been put to work on fortifications, but their behavior was disquieting, largely by reason of their own claim that they were "prisoners of war." They did not come as servants. They were people who had been forcibly dispossessed. Perhaps no other colony could have handled the matter as South Carolina finally did. In 1712 the care of the poor had been put under the charge of vestries and churchwardens, so, when the Acadians became charity cases, the obligation for their keep became largely an item of parish administration. The French Huguenots had settled along the Santee River, so it is not surprising to find

Acadians sent to Prince Frederick Winyah. The vestry books of this parish record a number of large families apportioned among the regular parishioners.[47] On April 4th, 1759, over £3,000 was allowed for maintenance of "the French Acadians," two-thirds of this went to the church wardens of St. Philip's, Charles Town.[48]

A measure was passed on July 6, 1756, for their dispersal and indenture. Only one-fifth were allowed to remain in Charleston; the others were to be divided among the several parishes. "Indenture would provide a cheap means of furnishing subsistence and compelling work and would give the colony an additional, if not a very effective, labor supply."[49]

CHAPTER IV

Sources of Supply

AFTER CONSIDERATION OF THE VARIOUS REASONS for introducing white servants, attention should next be given to the sources from which they were drawn. Disbanded soldiers, defeated rebels, orphans, convicts, destitute Irish, and poor Protestants made up the more important contributing groups. In 1697 the Council of Trade and Plantations was concerned whether the King would "be pleased to be at the charge of transporting any disbanded soldiers" to the colonies. The end of the war in Europe should have provided an opportunity at this time for new servants. If the King were not interested, "it remains only that those who are willing to be transported as servants for a certain number of years apply to the merchants dealing with the said Plantations, and make their own terms with them beforehand." [1] If none came out after the Peace of Ryswick, the government undertook a great experiment in Nova Scotia after the 1748 peace.

If victorious English soldiers were not available, defeated English and Scottish rebels were. There was generally a plentiful supply to be found among the adherents of the lost cause in the civil strifes of the mother-country.[2] During the assizes held by the notorious Judge Jeffreys after the failure of Monmouth's Rebellion, wholesale deportation became the order of the day. Under date of September and October 1685 appear numerous lists of rebels to be transported from Dorchester, Taunton, Wells, and Exeter.[3] Parliament passed a law arranging for transportation which required the colonies to pass laws for receiving them. On January 8, 1687, Lieutenant Governor Stede of Barbados wrote the Lords of Trade and Plantations: "We have already passed the Act required respecting transported rebels, which I hope will meet with approval. The first ship-load of them has arrived, and I send an account of the people to whom they have been assigned. A second shipload does not agree with the list sent to me." [4] After the Revolution of 1688 the King "ordered the law concerning transported convicts of Monmouth's rebellion to be repealed." [5] It is not certain whether any of these came to Carolina but some of the defeated Highlanders did come out to Carolina after the suppression of the rebellion in 1715.

Convicts were among those brought out to Carolina as servants. An advertisement was run in the *Gazette* during the fall of 1739 for two runaways from Virginia.[6] Two years later Robert Elicot, "a convict felon," was advertised for in the same newspaper.[7] One report from Georgia referred to Thomas Wright, "a transported convict," who had gone with several traders to Carolina.[8] Yet, on the whole, the average servant in South Carolina was perhaps of a higher type than those in the other colonies; at least, the leaven of social outcasts was remarkably few as far as the records of the colony indicate.

Attempts were made in other colonies to prevent the entry of such people. In 1670 an "Order of the Gen. Ct. held at Jas. City" in Virginia set forth "the danger to the Colony caused by the great number of felons and other desperate villains sent over from the prisons of England" and prohibited "the landing of any jail birds from and after 20th January next." [9] In 1672 Jamaica declared that "Whereas divers thefts, felonies and other enormities have been committed lately on Port Royal, which cannot be imputed to anything but the greater number of malefactors and other convicts yearly brought from his Majesty's prisons in England," it is ordered that every ship's master bringing such "shall report the number brought, and provide sufficient security that they would not be sold, or remain in Port Royal." [10]

South Carolina passed a law in 1712 providing for a fine of "Twenty five Pounds Currant Money" to be collected from the "importers of such servants, or the masters of ships which should bring them over" for "each Criminal out of Newgate or any other Gaol of Great Britain." [11]

In 1726 there was evidence of a committee being appointed by the House to wait on Captain Stewart "to tell him that he should be obliged to produce proper certificates from the Mayor of Bristol that they [his immigrants] are not convicts. . . ." [12] In spite of what was surely a warning, Captain Stewart brought in two years later among his emigrants eighteen men and six women sentenced to seven years for felony.[13] The problem was obviously one too difficult to control from the colonial side. In February 1741 it was proposed to add to the bill for governing and regulating white servants, a clause "to prevent convicts being brought into this Province." [14]

An interesting incident which serves to show the practically unanimous opposition to women convicts was the attempt to dispose of fifty such malefactors by shipping them to one of the colonies. On July 1, 1697, the Lords Justices apprised the Council of Trade and Plantations, "There are about fifty women convicts now lying in Newgate for transportation." The Council was requested "to report to what places these women should be sent." [15] New England virtuously excused herself, the agent for Massachusetts referring to the colonial government which had "from their first settlement earnestly desired to be excused from entertaining criminals. But," he added, "it is well known that they will be willingly entertained by Virginia, Maryland, Barbados, Jamaica or the Leeward Islands." [16]

The agent for Virginia states that that colony and Maryland "being on the Continent and several Governments joining on each other have found the entertainment of convicts to be prejudicial and have passed a law against the importation of them. There will therefore be no proper place but Jamaica and Barbados, who will bid them welcome, as they most properly may, being confined under one Government and enclosed within the Island." [17] Jamaica declines, but on different grounds; she needs men for field work, and her merchants inform the Council that they "would not receive them [the women] except on condition of receiving one hundred and fifty male convicts with them." [18] The agents for Barbados feel, "It will be no convenience—but in places where white women work in the field, as Virginia and Carolina, such women as those may be useful and acceptable." [19]

On July 9, 1687, William Thornburgh wrote to William Popple, who had sent the letter of inquiry to the agents of the various colonies: "I cannot yet arrange a meeting of the Lords Proprietors of Carolina to consider your letter respecting women convicts, but you may be assured that the Proprietors will acquiesce in the Lords Justices' pleasure if they transport them to Carolina. What reception they will find there I cannot say, though it will be better than elsewhere, for most of the rest of the West Indian settlements (if not all, to my certain knowledge) will not receive women convicts. If you resolve to send them to Carolina, I have a ship bound thither that will carry them at the usual rates, and the master will be careful to procure for them the best reception he can." [20]

Thornburgh was obviously more interested in a profitable cargo than in the good of the colony. The Proprietors must have over-ruled him, for none were sent to that colony. On July 21 the matter came up before the commissioners on transportation when the answers from the agents of the colonies were read, and since all refused to receive these women except the Leeward Islands, it was agreed to recommend that they be sent thither. Such an order was issued by the Lords Justices on the twenty-ninth. [21]

The destitute Irish represented another important source of serv-ants. The presence of large numbers of destitute people at home had provided a supply, especially in the early 17th century when the economic writers still felt England to be overpopulated. With the coming of the industrial revolution, ideas about overpopulation changed. There was less reason to believe that England was over-populated and therefore the destitute Irish became a principal source of indentured servants for the colonies. Many of these servants were carried out to the colonies by merchants looking for an outward-bound cargo, simply to make money out of their passage rather than to sail in ballast. The bulky products, of course, were those carried on the homeward-bound voyage: the sugar, rice, and tobacco of the southern colonies.

The arrival of these Irish servants was often advertised in the *Gazette*. An example was the notice of men and women servants from Dublin, aboard a ship in the harbors, among whom were "some tradesmen." [22] Merchants were not always responsible for their coming, although usually they acted as intermediaries. Samuel Wyly, for instance, brought servants over who had been indentured to him in Ireland. [23] Hugh Cunhary and Cornelius Melone and wife arrived in that situation about 1751 and four years later they had served their time and were given lands in Craven County and on Wateree River at the mouth of Twenty-five Mile Creek respectively. [24] Wyly, incidentally, became a trader on Pine Tree Creek, later the Camden area. Other instances were Denis Hagen, bound to Robert Belton in Ireland, 50 acres in Craven County, 1755; [25] and John Dowling, bound to Robert Milhous in Dublin for four years, was given fifty acres on the Santee River "or the waters thereof," 1755. [26]

The mercantile firms, as importers of servants, were not too careful about their treatment, as the more important purpose of the
transaction was to get ships over to South Carolina which could
carry local produce back to Europe. Consequently, the Irish—as well
as others—suffered greatly. This was particularly true during the
period when slave importations into Carolina had been prohibited.[27]
It was almost as if the British merchants had redirected their vessels
from the African coast to the Irish coast, with the white servants
coming over in much the same fashion as the African slaves.
Nathaniel Russell described in 1767, just after coming to Charles
Town as agent for Rhode Island merchants, the barbarous conditions
under which the Irish were brought in.

> About six weeks past a ship arriv'd here from Belfast with a
> number of passengers the owners or merchants there being very
> anxious to procure as many passengers as possible. Instead of
> two hundred (Which was the most they could bring with
> comfort) they brot out 450 & their agreement was for 19 inches
> room in width for each person but they scarcely had seven,
> their being so much crowded and the bad usage they met with
> from the master of the ship who cut them off in their allowances
> of Provis almost three Quarters brot on a distemper which
> carried off upwards of a hundred on the passage. The survivors
> were in a most pitifull condition when they arrivd here There
> were many parents who buried all their children & many chil-
> dren without Parent Friend or Relation. As soon as they Landed
> they were ordered into the Barracks The Church Wardens
> immediately carried about subscriptions to raise a sum of money
> for their relief & in two days had upwards of two hundred
> pound sterling subscribed exclusive of Blankets, Linen, Cloaths,
> & every necessary that the sick & naked stood in need of.[28]

Henry Laurens, as agent for certain Bristol and Glasgow merchants, was receiving some of these poor Irish immigrants and did
not relish his business. On January 26, 1768, he wrote: "The Irish
Servants have been a great plague to me & I am sorry that they
were so put on board the Wambaw; they are not worth their homony
to me." [29] Again a month later he advised a Bristol correspondent:
"I shall do the best in my power—with the Indented servants—
from whom I expect no great profits to arise." [30] In March, he
complained to a Glasgow firm that he was having all kinds of
trouble with servants sent by them, being threatened with law-suits
because of evil treatment they had received on the voyage over.[31]

At the same time he wrote Bristol merchants that he would dispose of the rest of their servants "in the best manner in my power, but I fear they will dispose of themselves by running away into the Country, from whence it will not be worth bringing them back again." [32] The next month, he had "made an end of the account of the servants by giving them away to save great expense." [33]

Rather different from this situation was that when certain indentured servants were sent over to South Carolina for specific reasons. An example is described in a letter from Captain George Lucas to his daughter, Eliza, in the 1740's:

> I send by this Sloop two Irishe servants, viz, a Weaver & a Spinner, Indentured her at 10 Sterling per Annum, & as I am informed Mr. Cattle has produced both Flax & Hemp I pray you will purchase some of the latter and order a loom and spinning wheel to be made for them, and set them to work, but lest it should not to be had in Carolina I shall order Flax to be sent from Philadelphia with the seed, that they may not be idle. I pray you will also purchase wool and Sett them to making negroes Cloathing which may be sufficient for my own People and the overplus to be sold. I have also agreed with two more women Spinners and a man Labourer (who I found inclined to go to Carolina) to pay their Passages which is four pounds four shil. this Currency each, they to serve any master or mistress inclin'd to employ them and out of their wages to repay you the said sums, or to serve me a year unless they can otherwise raise money to pay their Passages.[34]

Apparently, the above example is an exception due to the personal concern involved, but the general lot of servants was usually described as worse than that of the slaves.

CHAPTER V

The Poor Protestants of Europe

By FAR THE LARGEST NUMBER and certainly the most important group of the white indentured servants were the poor Protestants from Europe. These were largely voluntary immigrants, seeking to escape a condition become intolerable at home because of economic, religious, and political oppression. As these conditions were more or less prevalent in all parts of the European world, there was a sprinkling of many nationalities among the colony's servant class. Of course, since the Catholics were discouraged from coming, the immigrants were representative of the northern Protestant nations. After a search of the *Gazette* the following breakdown of nationalities can be made: [1]

TABLE IV
Nationalities of Servants

German (including Dutch)	29
Irish	25
English	21
Scotch	15
Welsh	7
Swiss	4
French	4
Portuguese	3
Scotch-Irish	2
Virginian	2
New Englander	1
Norwegian	1

The individual references were as follows:

Nationalities Represented among White Servants: Names Appearing in the Gazette

Dutch:

Johannes Henric Bokker	June 5th and 12th, 1755
John George Coone	Aug. 12th, 19th and 26th, 1745

TABLE IV—*Continued*

Johannes Stephen Ellizer . . . . May 28th, June 4th and 25th, 1750
Henry George Fowser . . . . Oct. 31st and Nov. 7th, 1754
Conrade Minky . . . . May 20th and 27th, 1751
Mary Ann Moyer . . . . May 15th, 22d and 29th, 1742
Michael Muck . . . . May 20th and 27th and June 3d, 1751
Johannes Pacer . . . . April to June, 1753
Johanes Paul . . . . Sept. 3d, 10th and 17th, 1753
John Procey . . . . May 28th, June 4th and 25th, 1750
Nicholas Rhodmyer . . . . Feb. 1st and 8th, 1768
Dorothy Seitson . . . . Oct. 29th, Nov. 5th and 16th, 1753
Feyt Steogstyeber . . . . March 25th, April 1st and 8th, 1745
Jacob Stout (or Stall) . . . . March 25th, April 1st and 8th, 1745
George Michael Waller . . . . June 5th and 12th, 1755
Conrad Webber . . . . Aug. 16th, 23d and 30th, 1773
Andrew Wingler . . . . March 25th, April 1st and 8th, 1745

(Hollander):
Richard Aalder . . . . Aug. 9th and 23d, 1773

English:
Robert Allen . . . . Aug. 16th, 23d and 30th, 1742
Langham Booth . . . . March 5th, 12th and 19th, 1750
John Boyer . . . . Aug. 20th and 27th, Sept. 3d, 1744
Ann Brown . . . . Jan. 19th and 26th and Feb. 2d, 1738
Wm. Clows (or Clews) . . . . March 13th, 20th and 27th, 1736
Joseph Fillow . . . . March 3d, 10th and 17th, 1746
James Hannah . . . . June 11th, 18th and 25th, 1735
George Haworth . . . . March 5th, 12th and 19th, 1750
Joseph Holloway . . . . Dec., 1742 and Jan., 1743
Sarah Logge . . . . July 2d and 9th, 1737
William Loyd . . . . Oct. 27th and Nov. 3d, 1746
William Madame . . . . Aug. 17th and 24th and Sept. 1st, 1752
William Merick . . . . April 14th and 21st, 1733
Richard Owen . . . . Feb. 13th, 20th and 27th and March 5th, 1744
John Robinson . . . . Feb. 19th and 26th and March 5th, 1741
Charles Turner . . . . Nov. 12th, 19th and 26th, 1750
Joseph Waters . . . . Sept. 10th, 17th and 24th, 1744
Thomas Watson . . . . March 12th, 19th and 26th, 1744
John Whillingham . . . . March 5th, 12th and 19th, 1750

TABLE IV—*Continued*

John Willis .... June 5th, 14th and 21st, 1742
Samuel Wright .... Aug. 17th and 24th and Sept. 1st, 1752

French:
Tobias Chop .... Jan. 6th, 13th and 20th, 1757
John Daniel .... Sept. 10th, 17th and 24th, 1753
John Fougasse .... Jan. 29th, Feb. 5th, 12th, 19th and 26th, 1750
Espare Lamare .... Sept. 10th, 17th and 24th, 1753

German:
Christian Findling .... Jan. 15th, 22d and 29th, 1753
Yerick Groener .... Jan. 23d and 30th, Feb. 6th, 1755
Mark Hermon .... Jan. 23d and 30th, Feb. 6th, 1755
John Lowerman .... Jan. 8th and 15th, 1754
Jacob Prupacher .... Oct. 10th and 17th, 1754
Anthony Snell .... Jan. 25th, Feb. 1st and 8th, 1768
David Ludowick Thomas .... Jan. 23d and 30th, Feb. 6th, 1755
Robert Traut .... Jan. 8th and 15th, 1754

(Palatine):
Philip Schaffer .... March 5th, 12th and 19th, 1750
Johannes Schollar .... March 5th, 12th and 19th, 1750

(Wirtemberger):
Adam Algier .... Feb. 12th and 19th, 1756

Irish:
Luke Blakely .... April 8th, 15th and 22d, 1745
John Boyle .... Feb. 11th, 18th and 25th, 1745
John Brooks .... Feb. 26th, March 5th and 12th, 1741
Walter Brozock .... Feb. 11th, 18th and 25th, 1745
William Bulkley .... Feb. 12th, 19th and 26th, 1741
John Carroll .... May 16th and 25th and June 1st, 1748
Lawrence Colman .... Nov. 14th, 21st and 28th, 1741
Robert Cunningham .... Feb. 7th, 14th and 21st, 1736
Patrick Dwyero .... Feb. 24th, March 3d and 10th, 1733
John Field .... Aug. 8th, 15th and 22d, 1741
Thomas Field .... June 22d and 29th, 1734
John Fitxpatrick .... June 4th, 11th and 18th, 1741
Barnard Hughs .... March 5th, 12th and 19th, 1737

TABLE IV—*Continued*

Peter Laurens ....Feb. 7th, 14th and 21st, 1736
Richard Lee ....June 22d and 29th, 1734
John Maccarry ....Feb. 19th and 26th and March 5th, 1741
James Machone ....June 10th and 17th, 1732
James Mogra ....Feb. 26th, March 5th and 12th, 1741
John Murphy ....Feb. 11th, 18th and 25th, 1745
Thomas Ryan ....Aug. 17th, 24th and 31st, 1734
John Spring ....March 29th and April 5th, 1735
Walter Welch ....April 9th, 16th and 23d, 1741
William Welsh ....June 10th and 17th, 1732
James Whelan ....Feb. 12th, 19th and 26th, 1741
Robert Whitaker ....July to September, 1751

New Englander:
James Hewitt ....Aug. 4th, 11th and 18th, 1733

Norwegian:
Paul Christian Wolf ....April 15th, 22d and 29th, 1751

Portuguese:
Manuel Lozenfo ....Feb. 19th and 26th and March 5th, 1741
"a man and his son" ....May to August, 1742

Scotch:
Andrew Adams ....March 12th, 19th and 26th, 1744
Robert Broke ....April 14th and 21st, 1733
Alexander Crombie ....Nov. 13th, 20th and 27th, 1736
James Cupit ....Feb. 12th, 19th and 26th, 1737
George Dempster ....June 29th, July 6th and 13th, 1734
David Dundie ....Jan. 30th, February, March 5th, 1744
Hugh Forbess ....June 29th, July 6th and 13th, 1734
George Lesley ....Jan. 19th and 26th, 1738
Jane Mackenzie ....Dec. 3d and 17th, 1753
John Montgomery ....Nov. 21st and 28th and Dec. 5th, 1743
Tho. Straughan ....March 12th, 19th and 26th, 1744
John Thompson ....Nov. 16th, 23d and 30th, 1734
James Todd ....Oct. 26th, Nov. 2d and 9th, 1734
James Turnbull ....June 29th, July 6th and 13th, 1734
Walter Wallace ....April 5th, 1735

TABLE IV—Continued

(Scotch-Irish):

Roger O Mony .... March 22d and 29th, April 5th, 1735
Alexander Sinkler .... March 22d and 29th, April 5th, 1735

Swiss:

Nicholas Bony .... April 9th, 16th and 23d, 1737
John Peter Bovet .... Dec. 23d and 30th, Jan. 6th, 1732-3
Casper Morgendaler .... April 9th, 16th and 23d, 1737
Barthol Topler .... April 9th, 16th and 23d, 1737

Virginian:

John Swinny .... Aug. 17th and 24th and Sept. 1st, 1752
Samuel Ward .... Feb. 2d, 9th and 16th, 1734

Welsh:

Owen Bowen .... April 20th and 27th, 1734
Thomas Edwards .... Feb. 7th, 14th, 21st, 28th, 1743
Jenkin James .... June 16th, 23d and 30th, 1739
Dorothy Morgan .... May 28th, June 4th and 11th, 1750
John Richards .... June 22d, 1745
Ruth Willcock .... June and July, 1742
Patrick Welsh, alias John English who, according to the *Gazette*
(August, 1737), talks Spanish and Portuguese.

The largest group represented outside of the British Isles were the
Germans. Many of these Germans came as redemptioners. The redemptioner after his arrival in America was on the same level as the
white indentured servant. The difference between the two came in
considering the possibilities for getting to America. It was customary
"to supply an indentured servant with food, clothing, and shelter from
the time he signed his contract until the end of his term of servitude."
Therefore destitute persons in Britain found this a means to get free
of their worst immediate troubles. White indentured servants therefore usually came singly. The redemptionist system applied more to
whole families bringing their goods and chattels with them and seeking a new home. Redemptioners were apt to be people who had raised
some money by the sale of their lands or other non-movable property. Sometimes parents would come with the expectation of selling
the service of their children in order to pay for the passage of the

family, the children becoming apprenticed and thereby learning a trade. The white indentured servants came from Britain and came earlier; the redemptionists came from the continent and came later.[2]

Writing on the "Redemptioners and Indentured Servants in the Colony and Commonwealth of Pennsylvania," Geiser has made the following summary, which is applicable to South Carolina: "From 1682 to 1708 the proportion of servants to the whole number of immigrants was about one-third; from 1708, with the increase of Germans, to 1728, a period in which they were impelled by the wars of Europe, the proportion of servants increased to about one-half the number of immigrants. From 1728 to the end of the century, the great majority of Germans which constituted the main current of foreigners into Pennsylvania were redemptioners. The Scotch-Irish who formed a considerable portion of the immigrants from the beginning of this period to the middle of the century, came under almost the same force of circumstances as the early Germans and, like them, after they had established themselves, invited their friends who were in poor circumstances, and paid their passages, in return for which the immigrants bound themselves." [3]

There was no stigma attached to thus providing for transportation of the family. In "A Brief Description of the Province of Carolina on the coasts of Florida," which appeared in 1708, the privileges to be gained are thus set forth:

Let no man be troubled at the thoughts of being a Servant for 4 or 5 year, for I can assure you, that many men give mony with their children to serve 7 years, to take more pains and fare nothing so well as the Servants in this Plantation will do. Then it is to be considered, that so soon as he is out of his time, he hath Land and Tools, and Clothes given him, and is in a way of advancement. Therefore all Artificers, as *Carpenters, Wheelrights, Joyners, Coopers, Bricklayers, Smiths,* or diligent Husbandmen and Labourers, that are willing to advance their fortunes, and live in a most pleasant healthful and fruitful Country, where Artificers are of high esteem, and used with all Civility and Courtesie imaginable, may take notice, that, . . . "an opportunity offers now . . . [Moreover] If any Maid or single Woman have a desire to go over, they will think themselves in the Golden Age, when Men paid a Dowry for their Wives; for if they be but Civil, and under 50 years of Age, some honest Man or other, will purchase them for their Wives." [4]

The advertisements of the day must have tempted many persons to leave their homes. On November 28, 1717, Governor Robert Johnson sent the House a letter from a Mr. Wilson, a merchant in Belfast, suggesting that some action be taken to provide him against loss in a venture he had made. When Wilson had begun negotiations, Carolina money had been computed at a higher value sterling, by fifty per cent. Now having secured his immigrants, he stood to lose. The sum of £837 current money was promised him by the legislature to cover him against his loss.[5] There were many such ventures on the part of individual speculators. Alexander French delivered to the Committee of Petitions and Accounts on March 3, 1725, proposals "for bringing in and settling a number of good Industrious Inhabitants from Europe."[6] In 1726 Charles Hill applied for a copy of the late "Law for incouragement of White people to come into this Province" which he proposed to have translated into "Dutch" and then distributed throughout the Palatinate.[7] Yet many of these must have found themselves forced, as did 200 Palatines in 1735, "to sell themselves and their Children for their Passage (which is six Pistols in Gold per head,) within a fortnight from the time of their arrival, according to the Agreement they made with the Captain. . . ."[8]

The emigrants were quite often lured to one of the German or Dutch ports where, through the failure of funds, they were obliged to put themselves into the hands of one of the many rival promoters. In 1749 John Jacob Riemensperger set forth, in a petition to the Governor and the two Houses, "That the Petitioner on the encouragement given him by this Government went to England, from that to Holland, and thence up into Germany and Switzerland. . . . That the Petitioner . . . did actually procure and engage upwards of three thousand Persons to be willing . . . to come into this Province." During this absence in search of funds, "the greatest number of them ventured to come as far as Holland, in hopes of meeting either with the Petitioner, or some order for their being provided for, of both which being disappointed, and many of them not being able to support themselves in Holland, the greater and richer part of them were prevailed upon by Mr. Headman, of Rotterdam, to go in some Vessels of his into Pensilvania. . . ." Still others of the number were induced to go to Georgia; yet "Notwithstanding . . . the Petitioner had still been so successful as to secure upwards of six hundred for this Province." [9] Riemensperger was ready to bring these over if funds were provided.[10]

Governor Glen of South Carolina emphasized this group in his message of November 23, 1749: "Germany has been long the Seat of War, and has severely felt the calamities of it; and it may be presumed there are many of her People who wish for a place to rest, in which they may enjoy the fruits of their own labour, as many of their countrymen do here." [11] Ramsay, however, emphasized Irish immigration: "But of all other countries, none has furnished the province with so many inhabitants as Ireland. Scarce a ship sailed from any of its ports for Charlestown that was not crowded with men, women, and children. . . . Many causes may be assigned for this spirit of emigration from Ireland, but domestic oppression was the most powerful and prevalent." [12]

Governor Glen further described these redemptioners:

> The General Assembly, about two Years ago, (understanding that there was in the Treasury a considerable Sum of that Money appropriated by the General Duty Act, for the Encouragement of poor Protestants to become Setlers in the Province) passed an Act to increase the Bounty to be given to each; which is now four Pounds Sterling to all above the Age of twelve Years, and two Pounds to those who are between two Years and twelve, and one Pound to all under two Years; besides this, his Majesty's Bounty is one Hundred Acres of Land, wherever they chose it, provided it has not been granted before, to the Head of every Family, Male or Female; and fifty Acres for every Child, indented Servant, or Slave, the Family consists of. . . . If this Act has the desired Effect, the Security and Opulence of the Province will be increased, and the Adventurers will be pleased to find a Change from Poverty and Distress to Ease and Plenty; they are invited to a Country not yet half settled, where the Rivers are crouded with Fish, and the Forests with Game; and no Game-Act to restrain them from enjoying those Bounties of Providence, no heavy Taxes to impoverish them, nor oppressive Landlords to snatch the hard-earned Morsel from the Mouth of Indigence, and where Industry will certainly inrich them.[13]

Visiting a community in which the German Protestants had settled, Governor Glen was proud to remark further:

> Wheat is cultivated, with much Success, by the German Protestants, who are settled on the interior Parts of the Province; they would have been able to supply the Province with all the Flour we consume, by this Time, had they not been interrupted

by the Cherokee War. . . . These industrious People distil a palatable Brandy from Peaches, which they have in great Plenty; likewise from Potatoes, Indian Corn, and Rye.[14]

Prominent Charles Town firms developed the importation of the Germans into quite a business. In 1745 Mackenzie and Roche advertised the arrival of "the Ship *St. Andrew Robert Brown* Master, from *Rotterdam,* with 300 Palatines, amongst which are several Tradesmen and Farmers, also a great Number of young Men and Maids, the greatest part are indebted for their Passage and are willing to serve any Person inclinable to purchase their Time." [15] In 1751 Austin and Laurens advertised: "About 200 German *Passengers,* Amongst them are several handicraft Tradesmen and Husbandmen, and likely young Boys and Girls: They are to be indented for a term of Years, to any Person who will pay their Passages." [16] In 1752 Benjamin D'Harriette and John McCall announced: "A Vessel is just arrived from *Rotterdam,* with German Servants in good Health. Amongst them are Tradesmen of all sorts, which will be indented on reasonable Terms." [17] In 1753 Captain Ross was back with the *Elizabeth* "after a dangerous Passage (the Ship being very leaky and girthed round in several Places) . . . with upwards of 300 German Passengers, all in good Health, and 9 children born in the Passage." [18]

The most unfortunate were those disappointed in the definite expectation of finding friends in the colony who would pay the expense of their passage. They came not with the definite idea of serving, but on the chance that they would have to indenture themselves only if they were unlucky enough not to find those who had promised to assist them. Thus: "Hen: Rigby, House Carpenter and Joiner, his Wife & a Daughter are brought over into this Province, in the Snow *Loyalty, John Fowler,* Master, from *Liverpoole*: They say they have a Relation in the said Province named *Thomas Rothall.* This is therefore to give Notice to the said *Rothall* (if he is in this Province,) that unless their Passages from *Liverpoole* is immediately paid, the said *Rigby* will be sold as a Servant for the same, by *John Fowler*." [19] If Rigby was sold, this was an excellent example of a 'redemptioner' and undoubtedly this was not a unique situation.

There were many Charles Town houses engaged in this importing business: Marmaduke Peacock; Laroche, de la Villette and Montaigut; Glen and Cooper; John Savage and Company; Austin and

Laurens; Benjamin D'Harriette and John McCall; Inglis, Pickering and Wraxall; Edwards, Fisher and Company; Hutchinson and Grimké. There are no business papers of these firms, only the advertisements in the *Gazette*.[20] It was not only that these merchants made a profit on the importation of these servants that made the trade important, but as Henry Laurens wrote in 1755: "The Palatine Trade to America being stopt will deprive us of many Ships that Constantly resorted there & have been the Chief means for Years past of keeping down our Freights." [21] This trade therefore fitted rather neatly into the English mercantile system. The merchants had an article of commerce for the outward bound voyages from Europe and the colony itself gained settlers who would spark the growth of the colony and add to its posture of defense.

Each of the royal governors was given a set of instructions on his first going out to the colony. There were generally provisions in the instructions issued to the South Carolina governors urging them to sponsor the importation of poor Protestants. By the twentieth instruction to Governor Broughton he was to get financial aid from the colony for the poor Protestants arriving in the colony. The Assembly passed an act in 1732 appropriating £5,000 currency from the duties collected on Negroes to be used for seven years towards defraying the charges of laying out townships and for paying the passages of and for purchasing tools, victuals, and necessaries for the poor Protestants desiring to settle in the province.[22]

In February 1735 several recently arrived "Switzers" petitioned the Council "praying they may be released from their Engagements on Account of their Passage hither, and become Settlers in this Province." [23] The Council made such a recommendation to the House, to which the latter seemed willing to agree, "but to prevent any abuses that may ensue, have Entered into the Resolution herewith sent you, to which we desire your Hon. Concurrence." [24] The House had "Resolved on Considering His Majestys 20th Instruction to His Excellency the Governor relating to the Encouragement to be given to Poor Protestants, who are desirous to Settle in this Province, that it is the Opinion of this House, that the said Instruction is only to be extended to poor Protestants who are Freemen and not to Covenant Servants, who shall arrive in this Province, and that Such Covenant Servants are not by the said Instruction or by any Engagements the

Genl. assembly have enterd into, intitled to any benefit under the same, and that this House will not make any further Provision for any persons that Indent themselves for their Passage, nor for any other Protestants, but those that come over and arrive in the Province Freemen." [25]

The wording of this resolution proves that there were two classes of poor Protestants: those indentured before leaving the old country, and those leaving home freemen, but entering the colony as servants; in other words, both indentured servants and redemptioners. The colony seemed willing to help the latter more than the former, probably on the basis that they were more desirable immigrants. The redemptioners, of course, would be less of a financial drain on the colony.

The action of the assembly in 1735, however, was not conclusive, for three years later the same question came up again in a quarrel between the Council and the House. On February 4, 1738, the Council came around to the House viewpoint, concluding that "Agreable to His Majesty's Instructions and with a Saving Clause, Then it is our Opinion Mr. Commissary do acquaint them [the immigrants then petitioning] their best way is to Enter into Service without any more loss of time, or burthen to the Inhabitants of Charles Town." To this, the House replied: "As to any Instructions to be given to the Commissary in the matter of the Petitioners entring into Service, this House Apprehend they are not at all concern'd therein any further at present than to Say that had their Advice been followed there had been no necessity of Driving Freemen into a State of Servitude." [26]

There was less argument over the colony's supplying food and necessary equipment for those arriving in the province. In 1730 a "list of necessarys for Strangers to be Imported by Capt. Crokat" provided for each person above the age of twelve years: eight bushels of corn or peas; 200 weight of beef; 50 of pork; 200 of rice; one bushel of salt; one axe; one broad and one narrow hoe. Also one cow, one calf, and one young sow were to be provided for every five persons "with some powder and Shot as may be found necessary." [27] On January 31, 1734, Colonel Parris, the public treasurer, was ordered to provide eight hogsheads of corn, 2 of peas, two of salt, and 18 barrels of beef for the use of the Irish Protestants settled at Wil-

TO BE SOLD, on board the *George-Town* Galley, *Thomas Craftwaite* Mafter, lying at *Frankland's* Wharff, fundry *Englifh* SERVANTS, Men and Women, well recommended, amongft whom are Tradef- men, Hufbandmen, &c. indented for *Four Years*.

Run away, three white fervants lately imported, *viz.* on funday the 25th of *February, Langham ——, about 5 feet 9 inches high, and 19 years of age, thin and ——lexon'd.* And on funday the 4th inftant, *George Ha- ——, about 5 feet 6, and 35 years old, black hair, and well fet, —— a blue coat: And John Whillingham, about 5 feet 6, and —— years old, fair complexion'd, with a wig, fuftian frock and lea- —— breeches, and are all country fellows, who may be eafily known by their fpeaking broad of the county of Lancafhire. Whoever —— up and brings them to Charles-Town,* will not only do pu- —— fervice, but be well rewarded by JAMES REID.

Whereas the fubfcriber has not been able to get —— of two *Palatine* fervants, who came in the fhip *Griffin, —— Arthur, from Loudon,* and deferted from the fick quarters in *Charles Town,* one call'd *Johannes Schollar,* aged about 23 years, a fhort thick perfon, and *Philip Schaffer* (a huffar) pretty well fet and lufty. Early enquiry having been made in *Saxe-Gotha, Con- ——, &c.* where 'twas imagined they were gone, it's now fuf- —— they may be harbour'd at fome plantation not fo diftant as —— townfhips. If they, or either of them will return, or pro- —— payment of their paffage, it will be accepted: 10 *l.* reward —— intelligence where one or both may be found. Any one en- —— or harbouring either of the faid fervants after this notice —— be profecuted at law, by OTHNIEL BEALE, & Comp.

The arrival of servants was advertised in *Postscript to the South Carolina Gazette,* November 27th, 1749 (above). And when they ran away, the *Gazette* notified South Carolinians to be on the lookout for them.

This entry in Henry Laurens' *Letter Book* describes a trying episode with twenty-six white servants destined for Florida who jumped ship in Charleston; when Laurens wrote to William Penn in St. Augustine, only twelve were back on board ship.

liamsburgh.[28] In December 1734 an order passed the House for the payment to Mr. William Pinckney of the "sume of Thirty pounds current money of this Province for the hire of a store and kitchen to the Saltzburghers lately imported hither in Capt Henning." [29]

There was a fund during the rest of the colonial period which was appropriated for the use of new settlers and was raised by duties on the importation of slaves. On May 10, 1748, the "Committee on the Treasurer's Accounts" reported a balance in the fund of £11,572.[30]

The most pretentious scheme for bringing in servants was that of John Peter Purry. Purry went to England in 1724 and made an agreement with the Lords Proprietors to bring in 600 persons in return for a grant of 24,000 acres. The Lords Proprietors also agreed to pay the charges of their transportation from England to Carolina. On April 27, 1725, they granted to Monsieur Jean Vatt in Switzerland "the 24,000 acres in trust to be transferred to M. Purry when he should have fulfilled his part of the agreement." A number of Swiss emigrants gathered at Neuchâtel in 1726 in anticipation of moving to Carolina. The Lords Proprietors, however, failed to provide transportation. Some of these undoubtedly made their way to Holland, where they took passage in a ship under the command of Captain Omer, contracting with him for their passage to the colony. On the request of the Swiss that the colony pay for their passage, the Council and the House refused.[31]

On July 20, 1730, Governor Johnson recommended that M. Purry "be granted 12,000 acres for himself, free from all quit-rents." Purry was to settle 600 Swiss Protestants within six years.[32] In *A Description of the Province of South Carolina,* drawn up by Purry in Charles Town in September 1731, he tried to indicate how much in demand tradesmen were and how easy it would be to work off any contract entered into for passage. He wrote: "Artificers are so scarce at present, that all sorts of Work is very dear; Taylors, Shoemakers, Smiths, &c. would be particularly acceptable there. A skilful Carpenter is not ashamed to demand 30s. *per* Day besides his Diet; and the Common Wages of a Workman is 20s. *per* Day, provided he speaks English; and when a Workman has but 10s. *per* Day he thinks he labours for almost nothing, tho' he has his Maintenance besides. But this is Carolina Money." [33]

Purry drew up at this time a set of thirteen proposals which could be used as a guide by those intending to emigrate. He laid down the requirements for two methods: one for persons desiring to go as servants and one for those desiring to settle on their own account.

Proposals by Mr. Peter Purry of Newfchatel, for Encouragement of such Swiss Protestants as should agree to accompany him to Carolina, to settle a new colony—Charles Town
September, 1731

"There are only two Methods, *viz:* one for Persons to go as Servants, the other to settle on their own Account.

1—Those who are desirous to go as Servants must be Carpenters, Vine Planters, Husbandmen, or good Labourers.

2—They must be such as are not very poor, but in a Condition to carry with them what is sufficient to support their common necessity.

3—They must have at least 3 or 4 good Shirts, and a Suit of Clothes each.

4—They are to have each for their Wages 100 Livres yearly, which make 50 Crowns of the Money of *Newfchatel* in *Swisserland,* but their Wages are not to commence till the Day of their arrival in *Carolina.*

5—Expert Carpenters shall have suitable Encouragement.

6—The time of their Contract shall be 3 Years, reckoning from the Day of their arrival in that Country.

7—They shall be supply'd in part of their Wages with Money to come from *Swisserland,* till they imbark for *Carolina.*

8—Their Wages shall be paid them regularly at the end of every Year; for security whereof they shall have the Fruits of their Labour, and generally all that can be procured for them, whether Moveables or Imoveables.

9—Victuals and Lodgings from the Day of their Imbarkation shall not be put to their Account, nor their Passage by Sea.

10—They shall have What Money they want advanced during the Term of their Service in part of their Wages to buy Linnen, Clothes and all other Necessaries.

11—If they happen to fall Sick they shall be lodg'd and nourished Gratis, but their wages shall not go on during their Illness, or that they are not able to Work.

12—They shall serve after Recovery, the time they had lost during their Sickness.

13—What goes to pay Physicians or Surgeons, shall be put to their Accompt.

As to those who go to settle on their own Account, they must have at least 50 Crowns each, because their Passage by Sea, and Victuals, will cost from 20 to 25 Crowns, and the rest of the Money shall go to procure divers things which will be absolutely necessary for the Voyage." [34]

Purry went to Switzerland himself during the winter of 1731-32 to secure immigrants. His son wrote to a friend in Charles Town, May 10, 1732: "Sir, My Father is in Switzerland, where he has purchased a Number of People, and hath great Hopes to get a great many Free Men, besides Women and Children; he intends to come back with them the next Month, or in July, to be all imbarked for South Carolina."[35] The exact arrivals of these immigrants were noted by Purry himself in affidavits made out at the Charles Town customhouse:

> Novemr. 1st., 1732, out of the Ship Peter and James, Joseph Cornish Master—Sixty-one men, Women and Children.
> Decemr. 13th, 1732, Out of the Ship Shoreham, John Edwards Master—Forty two men, Women and Children.
> December 15, 1732, Out of the Ship Purrysburgh, Joseph Fry Master—Forty nine men, Women and Children, who are all Come here on the footing of Switz Protestants.[36]

These were sent to Purrysburgh on the banks of the Savannah River where they were shortly joined by others. In 1733 the Reverend Joseph Bugnion, minister at Purrysburgh, got £350 from the assembly to assist him in bringing in 300 more Switzers.[37] The *Gazette* of April 26, 1735, contained excerpts from a letter from Purrysburgh of April 10 giving the information that "of 200 Protestant Swiss who were to embark in London" for Purrysburgh "100 have been put a shore in Georgia by Capt. Thompson" and they had arrived in the town.[38] Others continued to come: "On Sunday last arrived here Capt. *Hugh Percy* in 9 weeks from *Rotterdam* and 6 from *Cowes,* with 250 *Switzers* on board, who are come to settle a Township on the King's Land in this Province upon the Encouragement granted to other Foreigners. Amongst them are Ninety fit to bear Arms, and it is not doubted but their settling in this Province will much contribute to its Strength.[39] The purpose of the township fund had been, of course, for the building up of the frontier communities as an added measure of protection for the colony.

The following bill of charges against the sinking fund which had been provided out of the public treasury for the account of new settlers refers to the Purrysburgh project:

Dr. The Sinking Fund in South Carolina:

Surveying 9 townships . . . . £	4,500.
Present to Col. Purry Charges to S. C. & back to Eng.	300.
£400. Stg. gratuity to settle Purrysburg . . .	2,800.
Lodging & Provisions his people while in Chtown	500.
Yr's provision for 300 people above 12 yers. (@ £22.10)	6,750.
8 months for same	4,500.
Yr's provision for 100 under 12 yrs. (@ £11.5s.)	1,125.
8 months for ditto	750.
Axes, Hows, Saws, Powder & Shot	600.
Cattle, Hogs &c.	400.
Plats, grants, & fees	2,000.
Present of cattle & embarking first settlers for Ga.	2,000.
To Ga. per Act appr'g 3d Gal on Rum to raise	8,000.
Bldg Forts &c	8,500.

£42,725.[40]

The project for settling Purrysburgh was probably the largest of its kind, but certainly not the only one. In November 1732 James Pringle and other Irish Protestants petitioned the assembly to pay for their passages. The assembly decided: "Upon considering the Petition from the Irish lately arrived here it is the Opinion of this Board that if they will Settle in a Township according to His Majty's Instructions and as the Swiss have done they shall have like encouragement." [41]

Allowances at other times were given to Mr. Gordon and forty Scottish Highlanders for settling in one of the northern townships and to Mr. William York with sundry Palatines from Philadelphia. The latter had undoubtedly come on to South Carolina since Pennsylvania had adopted new taxes on servants entering that state.[42]

The following list of immigrant ships and parties will also serve to indicate the strength of the influx of German-speaking settlers from 1732 to 1752. The list is taken from a short work by Gilbert P. Voigt.

1732 Purry's first party. 45 Germans, largely if not exclusively Swiss.

1732 (Dec. 2) 50 Palatines expected.

1733 (July) 25 Salzburgers for Purrysburg.

1734 (November) 260 Swiss for Purrysburg. Some of these may have been German-Swiss.

1735 (July) 250 German Switzers.

1735 (July) 200 German Palatines.

1735 (July) 250 German-Swiss.

1736 (October) "A Great Number of German Swiss people." One hundred and seventy (?).

1737 (February) "Above 200 Switzers out of the canton of Tockenburgh (Toggenburg)."

1744 Captain Ham's ship, which brought over some Swiss from Bern, Ulrich Stokes from Chafhausen (Schaffhausen), and perhaps other settlers.

1744 Captain Abercrombie's ship with 260 or 300 Germans was captured by the Spanish. The settlers seem to have been released and allowed to proceed to Carolina.

1744 (December) Captain Brown's ship with 100 Palatines.

1749 (October) Ship "Griffin" with a "number of healthy Palatines."

1750 (January) Ship "Greenwich" with German servants.

1751 (November) Ship "Anne" with 200 Germans.

1752 (September) Ship with German servants.

1752 (October) Nearly 300 German servants.

1752 (November) Nearly 200 German servants.[43]

Despite the laws to provide for the settlement of poor Protestants and others in Europe, the immigrants did not come in as large numbers as the South Carolina government wanted.

In 1752, measures to increase inducements for more settlers were passed in the General Duty Act.

Three-fifths of the tax imposed on Negroes and other slaves, paid by the purchasers thereof, was to be applied for five years from the passing of this act to the payment of six pounds proclamation money to every poor Protestant from Europe, between the ages of twelve and fifty, who produced a certificate proving that he was a Protestant, and of good character; and payment of three pounds like money to every poor Protestant between the ages of two and twelve under the same circumstances, provided that they settled on any part of the southern frontier between Ponpon and Savanna rivers, or in the central parts of the province between Santee and Ponpon rivers, within forty miles of the seacoasts. These payments were to apply for the first three years after the passing of the act. For the remaining two years, four pounds proclamation money was to be paid to every poor Protestant between twelve and fifty, and two pounds like money to each one between two and twelve.

After the expiration of the term of five years, the three-fifths parts of the tax was to be appropriated for the payment of two pounds, thirteen shillings, and four pence proclamation money to every poor Protestant from Europe between the ages of twelve and fifty, and the payment of one pound, six shillings, and eight pence like money to every one between the ages of two and twelve, who settled in any part of the province during the continuance of the act. [44]

Some alterations were later made as the areas prescribed were apparently rapidly settled by new immigrants. Briefly, since a sufficient quantity of vacant lands for settling poor Protestants could not be found within the bounds limited for that purpose the sums of money appropriated by the tax mentioned were to be appropriated in this manner: five pounds proclamation money to be laid out in plantation tools or in tools proper for their respective occupations and corn or other provisions for every poor foreign Protestant from Europe then in the province who had not already received the said bounty, or who should arrive from Europe within four months from the time of the passing of this act, provided he was between the ages of twelve and fifty; and payment of the sum of two pounds and ten shillings like money in corn or other provisions for every such free poor foreign Protestant between the ages of two and twelve. "And likewise, for purchasing a Cow and Calf for every Five such poor Protestants as shall be settled together." And the like bounty for every poor Protestant from Europe who produced a certificate as mentioned in the previous act, provided he came over within the four month term. One moiety [half] of the bounty was to be given to the poor Protestant upon his demanding it, and the other moiety as soon as he was actually settled in any part of the province.

After the aforesaid bounties were fully satisfied and paid, then the sums of money thereafter arising from the tax were to be appropriated to the use of poor Protestants coming from Europe to settle in this province, after the rate of half the several sums per head allowed by this act to the Protestants for the original four months. The said half bounties were to be paid in the same manner as directed for whole bounties.[45]

Just before this act was passed the governor announced to the Council that

> . . . two Vessels are at present in this harbour with upwards of 800 foreign Protestants on board and 2 Others are hourly Expected with the like number . . . a Considerable Addition to our strength. . . .[46]

Other situations had not been as pleasant as is described in additional accounts in the councilor's journals.

Even after the law was passed providing additional funds for these Protestants, several months were required before it could be enacted into law as approval by Parliament had to be forthcoming. Meanwhile, the troubles of these poor people began to mount as shown in the incidents brought before the Council.

> Frederick Grunswig engaged German families to settle in the province. Two hundred fifty persons from Rotterdam. He planned to get some more, take them from Charlestown to . . . [western] land. He wanted to go over yearly and bring many Germans to settle here "for ever," and wanted to find a method "to defray the Expence of the Freight or hire a Ship for that purpose," or wanted the king to direct some shipping for that purpose "so that the people might immediately go on their lands."

Also a "Petition for encouragement to bring over German settlers and for Compensation for 250 persons already brought over"[47] was made; and Nathaniel Jones petitioned:

> That as the pet[r]. is favoured with a grant of land for his friends in Ireland and as he has taken upon him at his own hazard & Charges to settle those lands, and to bring over above 300 persons as the Pet. has but a small fortune and the undertaking attended with so considerable a charge by reason of the people's delays & unbelief of the place." Petitioner prays for eleven or twelve hundred bushels of corn and fifty or sixty hogs to be stored near the country, for he is sure that the people will come "since several have already sold their goods & places and others wait till they see the ships." He hopes wagons and horses will be ready to carry women, children, and baggage to the land.[48]

Andrew Seyer and Frederick Gronswick are going to Germany who can be Instrumental in procuring a Number of Foreign Protestants to come & Settle in this Province if they should be assured that they may have lands to set down upon when they arrive. We therefore desire that Your Excellcy. will be pleased to give the said Andrew Seyer and Frederick Gronswick assurances that such Forreign Protestants as shall come to settle here shall have lands upon their arrival & to give Your Excellcy the utmost assistance in our power, towards discovering such lands. We have appointed a committee to enquire where any vacant . . . lands may be ascertained & set appart for accomodation of Forreign Protestants who shall arrive here from Europe. . . .[49]

There being no money in the Fund for paying the Bounty to many poor Forreign Protestants lately arrived in this Province and who came hither upon the faith of the Public that such Bounty would be payed them and there being Large Sums of Public money in the Treasury as Ballance of Several Funds some of which I apprehend there is no Immediate Demand for I think it would be for the Benefit of the Public if some part of that money was Borrowed in order to pay off those poor People who have been Long Detained in Town for want of it and which may be Replaced before it can be Wanted and I the Rather Recommend this method to you as it is to be feared that Certificates from the Commissioners may be Counterfeited and were often sold by the Poor people possessed of them for Less than the Value.

James Glen
In the Council Chamber [50]

Petition of several poor German Protestants lately arrived from Rotterdam stated that:

The petitioners were invited to come with their families to this province, seeing papers dispersed in Germany to the effect that all who came and could free themselves should be entitled to 50 acres of land for each member of the family, and a bounty for a year's subsistance of 30 pounds. Some people returning to Germany from this country confirmed what the papers said. The petitioners, on first arriving in this province, owed considerable sums to the ships that brought them and had no right to apply for the bounty. Finally, the merchants to whom they were addressed, unable to get masters for the petitioners, resolved to discharge them upon their bonds to ease themselves of a heavy daily expence. The petitioners applied to the governor and council, who ordered their warrants made out and the bounty paid to them, but the Commissary General told them there was no money in the Township Fund, and they must wait for orders from the General Assembly how the money should be raised. The petitioners had sold everything they owned except their apparel, and would have starved if the ship's provisions had been refused them. They no longer have any right to the ship's provisions, so the petitioners are asking if they may go into the country to provide their lands, build themselves huts, and clear some ground before the planting season approaches.

> Geo. Sumpert, Reintich Kumer, and about thirty more German Protestants.[51]

A resolution of Commons House of Assembly to which the governor assented provided,

> That all the monies in the Fund appropriated by the June 14, 1751 act be paid by the Public Treasurer to the Commissary General for use of the foreign Protestants lately arrived. The monies to be replaced in the fund out of 3/5 parts of the Tax appropriated by the said act "to the use of such poor Protestants as shall come over to Settle in this province. . . Concurred to by upper house and sent back.   Nov. 25, 1752.[52]

Another entry explained,

> The Reverend Mr. Zubly a protestant minister of the gospel was admitted before his Excellency and the Council and acquainted the Board that four Germans forreigners who on the 7th Instant Petitioned for Land and Bounty and then had Declared themselves of the Romish Religion having since that time been visited by the said Rev. Mr. Zubly after several conversations on the subject of the Errors of the Church of Rome they Declared that they had renounced the said Errors and Embraced the protestant Religion.[53]   Nov. 28, 1752.

Jan. 31, 1753—Thos. Ross and ship Elizabeth arrived from Rotterdam with 319 Protestants on board from Germany.[54]

Petitions of passengers explained:

> The petitioners are all foreign Protestants who left their own county to settle in this province. A New Lander brought them a contract made to them in Rotterdam and signed by Nicholas Oursell, Merchant, and Oursell did not treat the petitioners agreeable to the contract. He kept them nine weeks in Rotterdam where many of them would have had money enough to pay their passages, but they were obliged to spend this money for their maintenance. Now they will have to be sold to pay their

passage. Nine of their chests have been lost and others broken open and robbed, and there have been other grievances, too tedious to mention. They are now in a strange country with neither money nor friends nor any way to help themselves, and they pray of the governor and council that justice may be done them.

Jacob Bord and 27 more foreign Protestants [55]

Also,

. . . that the said Nicholas Oursell promises to provide & have in Readyness one or more Ships for the said Germans, against their approach in Rotterdam in order to take them on Board & with the assistance of God depart for Carolina & the said Ship or Ships Shall have convenient Cabbins made Ready for their Lodgings to say a Cabbin of Six foot Long & Six foot Broad for every four grown Persons or whole freights.

The Said Nicholas Oursell promises to provide & put on Board the said Ship good wholesome & fresh provisions consisting of meat Bread Flower Barley, Peas, Beans, Cheese, Butter, vinegar molasses Beer & water. . . .

The Fire shall be allowed to burn from 6 o'Clock in the morning to 6 in the Evening that such as have Small Children may have the priviledge of Cooking. . .

We the Subscribers Passengers for our frieght & Victuals & Drink & our Baggage Promise unto Mr. Nicholas Oursell or his order to pay for as follows that is to say for any Person at age of 14 & upwards Shall pay a whole freight & from 4 to 14 years Shall pay only half Freight & those under four shall have their free Passage & such as are poor & not able to pay their passage to Mr. Nicholas Oursell in Rotterdam shall pay the Same in Carolina to the merchant to whom they shall be Consigned who shall give them time to seek a good Conveniency, etc.; also, if a passenger died before half the trip was over, his heirs should pay half fare; if he should die after half the journey, they should pay full fare.[56]

The contract was made in Rotterdam, January 3, 1752, and the petitioners listed several breaches. There was no beer, and instead of two gallons of water, they were soon reduced to one pint. More passengers were aboard than the leaky ship could contain. Passengers had to pump night and day; they had to lash the vessel round with ropes to keep it together and to keep it from sinking. The Attorney General promised to investigate the passengers' claims.[57]

Many other Protestants were stranded without funds, and efforts were made to help them.[58]

Under a new bounty act for 1761 many "poor Protestants" became interested and sailed to the province. A summary of this measure, passed July 25, 1761, follows:

> Whereas the Encouragement heretofore given to Poor Protestants to become Settlers in this Province hath not had the desired Effect," in the Treasury on September 29, there remained £57,575. 11s. 3d. of the tax appropriated by the General Duty Law for that purpose, and "the public is enabled to increase the Bounty to "such Settlers." The "said Three Fifths of Tax appropriated & Applied by the said Law as an Encouragement to Protestants to become Settlers in this Province" shall from now on be appropriated and applied thus: "Four pounds sterling or the value thereof in the Current money of this Province to discharge and Defray the Expence of the passage from Europe of every poor Protestant" who has not already received a bounty from the province, who arrives to settle from Europe within three years from the passing of the act, and who, if from Great Britain or Ireland, shall "produce a Certificate under the Seal of any Corporation," or a Certificate from the minister and church wardens of any parish or minister and elders of any church meeting or congregation of his good character (if above age twelve). "Sum of Two pounds sterling or the Value thereof in Currency" to any poor Protestant between the ages of two and twelve, and the "Sum of Twenty shillings sterling or the Value in Current money" to each one over two, to buy tools and provisions. The money for passages is to be paid by the Public Treasurer to the owner or master of the ship in which the Protestants came, unless the Protestants have already paid him, in which case *they* receive the money. The bounty for tools is to be paid directly to the poor Protestants. The Act of October 7, 1752, and paragraphs 6 and 7 of the General Duty Act, "as far as the same relate to the Applying and Appropriating the said Three Fifths of the Tax thereby imposed on Negroes and other Slaves" is repealed.[59]

Miss Janie Revill has compiled a list of many German, Irish, and French Protestants. All of the important groups that came in from February 19, 1763, through January 23, 1773, are listed below:

February 19, 1763—
    70 Irish petitions for lands in Boonesborough Township

January 13, 1764 ....89 poor Protestants from Ireland
January 24, 1764 ....150 poor Protestants from Ireland
March 2, 1764—
     45 Germans petition for lands in Belfast Township
April 18, 1764 ....81 French Protestants
December 24, 1764 ....56 German Protestants
January 31, 1765 ....306 Germans
February 27, 1765—
     59 Germans petition for land in Londonborough Township
December 4, 1765 ....80 Irish Protestants
February 13, 1766 ....192 Germans from Rotterdam
March 31, 1766 ....51 Irish
October 17, 1766 ....128 Germans from Amsterdam
October 17, 1766 ....155 Germans
October 26, 1766 ....47 Irish
February 27, 1767 ....172 Irish
May 28, 1767 ....227 Irish
June 22, 1767 ....439 Irish
September 1, 1767 ....201 Irish
December 12, 1767 ....48 Scots and Irish
December 22, 1767 ....414 Irish
January 5, 1768 ....352 Irish
January 12, 1768 ....268 Irish
February 13, 1768 ....231 Irish
February 23, 1768 ....238 Irish
March 9, 1768 ....23 French
July 8, 1768 ....16 French
November 19, 1772 ....73 Irish
December 1, 1772 ....35 Irish
December 1, 1772 ....30 Germans
January 6, 1773 ....418 Irish
January 23, 1773 ....48 Irish [60]

The evidence is thus plentiful that thousands of poor Protestants
came to Carolina as indentured servants or as redemptioners. In time
the immigrant hopes for a new start in life would have been fulfilled.
The favorable issue of the following petitions is proof of that:

Read the Petition of John Froely, a Protestant Swiss, showing
that the Petitioner came into this Country about 5 years ago,
on the Encouragement which is given by His Majesty to foreign
Protestants, and being then unable to pay for his freight, was
obliged to serve 4 years to Mr. Cattell, but as his Servitude has
expired, having a wife and 5 children, in all seven persons, prays
that 350 acres of land be laid out to him in Orangeburg Township, and that he may be allowed the usual Bounty. The Petitioner appeared before the Board, and producing a discharge of

his Indenture from Mr. Cattell, and having swore to the truth of the Allegations in the said petition, the prayer thereof was granted and the Deputy Secretary ordered to prepare a warrant and the commissary General to Pay the Bounty accordingly.[61]

Read the Petition of Jacob Ernest, a Protestant Pallatine, showing that the Petitioner came to this Country about twelve Months ago, on the Encouragement which is given by His Majesty tc foreign Protestants, but being then not able to pay for his passage was ever since obliged to serve Mr. Tellaback, and his time being now expired, having a wife and child, intends to settle in Saxe Gotha Township, therefore prays a Warrant may [be] issued for 150 acres of land to be laid out to him in the above Township and that he may have the usual Bounty. The Petitioner appearing and swearing to the truth of the Allegations in his said petition, the prayer thereof was granted and the Deputy Secretary ordered to prepare a Warrant and the Commissary to pay the Bounty accordingly.[62]

Read the Petition of Henry Long, a Protestant Swiss, showing that the Petitioner came into this Province on the Encouragement given by His Majesty to foreign Protestants, and not being then able to pay for his Passage, about 4 years ago he served on his arrival Mr. John Cordes all that time and being at present free from his said Service prays that 50 acres of Land be laid out to him, in Orangeburg Township, and that he may be allowed the usual Bounty. The Petitioner appearing and swearing to the truth of the Allegations in the said Petition, the prayer thereof was granted and the Deputy Secretary ordered to prepare a Warrant and the Commissary to pay the Bounty.[63]

The subsequent history of many other redemptioners is described in the Council Journals and elsewhere.

Matthew Row, wife, and one child after serving indenture to John Coming Ball received 160 acres between the Savannah and Santee rivers (July 6, 1752).[64]

Jacob Andrews Herman came over with Rev. John Christian Riemensperger, was bound out as cabin boy to Omar Villeponteaux who was drowned when their ship was cast away on the shores of Virginia. Herman then served as servant to Mr. James Jule for 16 months and was given permission to return to South Carolina. He was awarded fifty acres "in or about the Congres." [65]

John Boomer arrived "around 1745." He, wife, and all his children were bound out to various persons. After seven years Boomer "now out of his time" was given 50 acres in the "forks between Broad and Saluda Rivers." [66]

Michael Kalteisen (spelling varied) was bound out to John Clark, shoemaker at Ashley Ferry. At Clark's death his time was sold to Dr. Frederick Holtzendorph who discharged Kalteisen's "indenture for a consideration paid." Kalteisen was awarded fifty acres between the Savannah and Santee rivers, 1752,[67] but his subsequent activities concerned the city of Charles Town. He was wagon master general in the Cherokee War, 1760-61, and also in 1775. The next year he was commissary of military stores and at the time of his death, 1807, was commander of Fort Johnson in the Charleston harbor.[68] One of the last references to this sturdy patriot was on the occasion of General Christopher Gadsden's death in August, 1805.

> Captain Kalteison, the venerable commandant at Ft. Johnson, as soon as he was informed of the death of the general, had the colours of the fort hung in mourning, and fired a gun every ten minutes, from the morning of yesterday (August 29) until the body was interned (afternoon of August 30). The vessels in the harbor has their coloures half-masted throughout the day.[69]

John William Lizard was bound out to Mr. Mongen, watchmaker, transferred to John Ulrich Tobler and took up 50 acres on the Savannah River, 1752,[70] probably in Mr. Tobler's community of New Windsor.

Two hundred acres on the Savannah were also given to John Valentine Cloudy in 1752. He, his wife, son Tobias, and another child had come from Rotterdam and he had served time with the Honorable William Ball, Jun., Esq.[71] Matthew Row and his wife served out their indentures with John Coming Ball and were awarded 160 acres between the Savannah and Santee rivers.

Another immigrant was Elizabeth Dor. Saunders who had come over from Rotterdam. Bound out to Alexander McGregor and "by him convey'd to others," her time was purchased by Jacob Culp who married her. Her bounty was paid to Culp, along with 150 acres, 1752.[72] Probably this was Jacob Culp (also Kolb) member of an important and patriotic family in the Pedee area, as the notice further remarked that "Culp came into this province about six months since having lived in Pennsylvania and Virginia some time." [73]

During these years scores of other German redemptioners had served out their indentures and were given land. A sampling indicates the areas being settled at that time.

Craven County: Harman Rich, wife, and one child, 150 acres, 1756.[74]

Granville County: Andrew Baumler and wife, 100 acres, 1756;[75] Katherine Barbara Bunkmeyer, 50 acres 1755;[76] John Jacob Zahler, 50 acres, 1755;[77] Anna Croesmanin, fifty acres, 1755;[78] Ursula Fingerlin, 50 acres, 1755.[79]

Also in Granville County, were Anna Maria Mire, wife of John, 50 acres on the Saltketchers (Salkehatchie River), 1755;[80] Mary Ann Winegelerin, 50 acres on the Saltketchers, 1755;[81] Albert Akerman, wife, and one child, 150 acres "on or near" Salkehatchie River, 1754 (they had arrived in 1731);[82] and George Gardiner (a carpenter), wife, and their one-year old child, formerly bound to Rev. Mr. Joachim Zubly, 150 acres about the Salkcatchers, 1754.[83] In or near Purisburgh, also bound to Rev. Mr. Zubly, were Leonard Rhyuhower and wife who were given 100 acres, 1754.[84]

Farther up the Savannah River, on Stevens' Creek, but still in Granville County was Jacob Pright, wife, and Christopher, his twelve-year old son, who was given 100 acres.[85]

Elsewhere, John Adam Eyering, wife, and two children, found 200 acres in Castle Creek Swamp, 1755;[86] Conrade Vintinger, wife, and two children, 200 acres on Chinquapin Branch, 1755;[87] George Shebby, 50 acres in Caump Creek;[88] Conrad Schram, 50 acres in Amelia Township, 1755;[89] Christian Findling, 50 acres between the Savannah and Santee rivers, 1755, with 100 acres later on Duncan's Creek;[90] and Elizabeth Herr, 50 acres in the fork of the Broad and Saluda rivers, 1754.[91]

As to the large numbers of these redemptioners, such evidence may serve two purposes. Their dispersal into the backcountry, during and after "their time," would certainly indicate the larger proportion of settlers there had derived from the movement. Also, it would seem that a type of "western democracy," comparable to the Sons of Liberty in Charleston and the Tidewater would have developed by the time of the Revolution. This latter observation, however, may be questioned as many of the Germans in the interior preferred to remain loyal to the Crown rather than side with the Revolutionaries.

CHAPTER VI

Hiring of White Servants

IN TREATING OF THE CONDITIONS under which men and women served their time, the first point to be noted is the indenture itself. The provisions contained in these instruments are mostly general in nature, differing in that respect from the more detailed indentures of apprentices bound out to learn some particular trade or business. Note, for example, the considerable attention to details in the following apprentice indenture:

> this indenture made this Twenty Fifth Day of April in the Tenth year of the Reign of our Sovereign Lord George the Third of Great Britain, France & Ireland King &c, & in the Year of our Lord One Thousand Seven Hundred & Seventy. Witnesseth That Levi Swaine of all Saints Parish, County of Craven, Province of South Carolina, hath of his own free Will voluntarily & by & with the Advice & Consent of his Parents Placed & Bound himself Apprentice unto Thomas Harris of Parish of all Saints, County & Province aforesd, Planter to Learn the Occupation of Plantation Business, after the manner which the said Thomas Harris Useth & with him as an Apprentice to dwell, Continue & serve from the Day of the Date hereof unto the full end & Term of Six Years from thence next ensuing, & fully to be Compleat & ended during all which Term of Six Years, the said Apprentice his said Master well & Faithfully shall serve, his Secrets keep, his lawfull Commands Gladly do & Obey; Hurt to his said Master he shall not do nor Wilfully suffer to be done of others But of the same to the utmost of his Power shall forthwith give Notice to his said Master. He shall not do nor Wilfuly suffer the Goods of his said Master, to be embezzled or Wasted nor them lend without his Consent; Matrimony he shall not Contract, From the service of his said Master he shall not at any time Depart or absent himself without his said Masters Leave, but in all things as a Good & Faithfull Apprentice his said Master shall at all times serve, During the Term. And the said Master Obliges himself to find his said Apprentice, He performing the above, to find him sufficient Meat, Washing & Lodging & at the end of the said Term to

give him two Suits of Cloaths, a Horse, Saddle & Bridle & to give him a Heifer Yearling to be Considered as his own Property, & carry with him the Increase at the end of the said Term.[1]

The indenture of the "servant" is usually much simpler. The service to be rendered is covered by a general clause. The promise of secrecy as to the trade of the master is wanting. The marriage of the servant, his behavior and the equipment to be furnished him when he is out of his time are provided for by statute, and are not a part of the indenture. Thus, the indenture of "William ffags," dated June 21, 1671, promised seventy acres of land "according to the concessions of the Lords Proprietors." [2] And, under date of September 5, 1728, "David Swinton, Tobacco Spinner and Snuff-maker" agreed with "Robert Paterson Merchant in Glasgow—during the space of five years to serve in Such Service and imploym't as the said Robt. Paterson or his foresaids shall there employ him in according to the Customs of the Country & in like kind and consideration of wch said Service the said Robt. Paterson or his friends is to pay for passage to find & allow him meat, Drink, apparell & Lodging During the said term or time and at the End of the Same to pay unto him the ordinary allowance according to the Customs of the Country." [3]

Again, there appears the indenture of the "Apprentice and Servant." In general, such appear to be servants rather than apprentices, although at times the context alone must decide. The greater number of servants emigrating to South Carolina made their arrangements with either the ship's captain or her owners or agents. The case of James Deall appears in full in the records of the Probate Court, showing the original indenture and assignment by the ship's captain, after reaching Charleston.

The second party to this indenture was "Thomas Forster of London, Mariner." Deall bound himself "to ye said Thomas to serve him or his Assignes in ye Plantation of Carolina beyond ye seas for ye space of four years next ensuing ye Arrival of ye said Sert in ye said Plantation. And doth hereby Covenant well & truly to serve his said master or his lawfull Assignes." This instrument, dated January 27, 1698, was recorded April 10, 1701.[4] With it appears a copy of the certificate by the deputy register before whom the deposition was made,[5] and also the following assignment: "I

Thomas Foster for & in Consideration of ye Sum of fifteen pounds Currt money in hand paid & by me received of & from John Jones do Sett & Assign over unto ye said Jones all my right & title I have unto ye within mentioned Servt. by name James Deall, as witness my hand this Second of August, 1699." [6]

A most elaborate indenture was that between Thomas Massey of the borough of Southwark, a sawyer, and John Ashby, a London merchant. In addition to the usual stipulations, the former agreed to "Spend Such Time each day [as is usuall] for Men of his Condition . . . and [in Cace] of Sickness or otherwise ye sd Massey shall become uncapable or shall [Neglect] to performe Such worke . . . he oblidgeth himself[fe] [to Serve] . . . So much Time Lon[ger and above] ye Two yeares above Mentioned." Ashby was to pay the passage of both Massey and the latter's wife, "and in Consideracon of his Wifes Dyett & Lodging Whilst she Remanes in ye family . . . shee shall Acc[ord]ing to her abillity doe wtsoever she Can in the house at ye sd Plantation . . . until her husband hath ffinished ye sd Limited Service . . ." At the end of the term, Ashby was to have the refusal of Massey's service, "at the usual rates paid for such work." [7]

Trouble was early experienced by reason of the fact that servants without indentures were constantly arriving; and it became necessary to provide certain rules for such as came in before entering any definite indenture agreement. "For the avoiding of all fraud or any other difference that may happen between masters and servants, when servants doe arrive in this Province without Indentures or other contracts," it was enacted (ratification April 9, 1687) that all under the age of ten years serve till they are twentyone; under fifteen and above ten years shall serve seven years; above the age of fifteen, to serve five years. Servants arriving from Barbados or other American colonies must serve like terms "from and after their arrival . . . [hereafter] in this Province. . . ." The age was to be determined by the "Grand Councell, or any other by them appoynted." Their treatment was to be the same as that of any other servants, and "att and upon the expiration of theire terme of service, lymitted as aforesaid, one suite of Apparell, one barrel of Indian Corne, one Axe and one Hoe" were to be furnished. [8] In the Act of 1717, servants under sixteen years at the time of their arrival, and having no indentures, were to serve till twenty-one; and if above the age of sixteen years, for five years.[9] A bill of sale, illustrating the working of this statutory provision as well as suggesting the severity of its action upon the children involved, is of record, under date of February 5, 1725.

After reciting the provisions of the Act for cases where there was no indenture, this instrument continues:

> And Whereas Saml. Sproll in & by a Certain writing under his hand & Seal bearing date at Quigleyes point on the Sixth day of November in the year of our Lord one thousand seven hundred & eighteen did oblige himself to pay to Mr. William Willson four pounds Sterling for the passage of his two children Alexander & James with the Currt. Exchange in South Carolina or to give Indentures of them the said William Willson & he should Agree & whereas the Said Saml. Sproll did not pay to the said William Willson the said sume of four pounds Sterling but agreed that his said two Children should become Servts. for the Same till they Severally attained the Age of twenty one years; & whereas by Indorsement on the said Writing Obligatory the said William Willson did Assign unto the Honble. Ralph Izard Esqr. the said writing obligatory & all his Interest or Service or title of apprenticeship or Servitude to the said Alexander & James or either of them & all benefitt and advantage arising by the said obligation. Now Know Ye that the said William Willson & also the said Saml. Sproul & his said Children Alexander & James have personally been & appeared before the said Thomas Broughton & have all & each & every of them mutually Condescended & agreed that they the said Alexander & James Sproll and Each of them shall Serve the said Ralph Izard & his Assigns as a Servant untill they Severally attain to their respective ages of twenty one years & the said Thomas Broughton upon Information of the said Sam Sproll & view of the said Alexander and James doth judge and determine the said Alexander Sproll is about the age of Six years & the said James Sproll is about the age of four Years.[10]

CHAPTER VII

Regulation of White Servants

A LARGE SHARE OF THE LEGISLATION "governing and regulating white servants" deals with one phase or another of the runaway problem. The case of John Radcliffe occupies considerable space in the Journal of the Grand Council of the very early days; and his attempt to escape service seems to have been followed, as an example, by a large proportion of the servants who came after him. Radcliffe was charged with planning to desert the colony, and take with him to the Spaniards a number of followers. This element of treason possibly explains the attention given the case. He was eventually discharged on condition of the payment of the fees and charges incurred in his capture, confinement, and trial. If this was paid by his master, Radcliffe was to serve the latter an additional twenty-one months (five months lost by reason of his absence and sixteen to cover the above charges). As an alternative, he might serve each creditor a term proportional to the amount owed, in this case, he must afterwards serve his master twenty-one months.[1] About a year after this decision, his master John Foster paid the balance due, and Radcliffe was ordered to return to his service for twenty-one months in addition to the balance of his indentured time.[2]

In 1686, "An Act inhibiting the trading with servants or slaves" provided that absconding servants "shall for every day they shall soe absent themselves, serve twenty eight days to their master or mistresse, over and above the contracted tyme of servitude." [3] The penalty for continued absence was nearly doubled five years later, the provision then being that such servants "shall for every naturall day . . . serve one whole weeke, and for every weeke, if they shall att any one tyme soe long absent themselves, one whole year . . . over and above their contracted tyme. . . ." [4]

When the comprehensive Act of 1717 appeared, provisions were made for many details of the runaway problem. First, as to the penalty: the scale of increased servitude was one week added for every day's absence, "and so in proportion for a longer or shorter time, the whole punishment not to exceed two years over and above the time" of the previous indenture agreement. Moreover, in addition to this extended service, the cost of "taking up" the fugitive was made chargeable against him. At the same time, he was in a measure protected, for the master must take him before the next Justice of the Peace and take oath or prove by witnesses the length of absence and the cost of apprehension. Thereupon, the Justice should grant a certificate, on which the Governor and Council were to pass judgment.[5]

The Act of 1744 added the cost of "whipping and bringing home," and reduced the maximum additional service from two years to one. Also, the judgment of the Justice of the Peace as to the time to be served and the charges to be paid, "certified under the hands and seals of such justices, is hereby declared to be sufficient in law to bind every such servant or servants according to the tenor thereof."[6] A second and serious difficulty was provided for by the certificate of release to be issued to a servant when his time had expired. This he had to take to the nearest Justice, who was required by law to "endorse and attest the same without fee or reward,"[7] which should then be sufficient warrant to all persons, in proof of the servant's release.[8] This was as necessary for protection of the general public as for the servant, for "whoever shall entertain or harbour any servant running away from his master's service, and not having a certificate as aforesaid, shall pay to the master of such servant for every day and night two pounds current money, for all the time he shall harbour or entertain him, so that the whole exceed not treble the value[9] of the servant's time remaining to be served. . . ."[10] Provision was made, also, for cases of forged certificates;[11] and in 1744 it was stipulated that the person entertaining a servant "ignorantly" should be free from the fine.[12] As a further measure of protection, a penalty of forty shillings might be inflicted upon "any punchhouse keeper, vintner or other person whatsoever, [who] shall entertain any man's servant . . . [so that he] shall be drunk, trade or game during such time [that is, of the servant's identure]. . . ."[13] The law of 1744 fixed a maximum penalty of £4., and provided that such fines be divided between the poor of the parish and the informer.[14]

Running away in company with slaves was deemed a felony, and punishment without benefit of clergy should follow.[15] This is practically of a kind with the law of 1727, which made the stealing of pettiaugers and Negroes a felony.[16] Persons taking up runaways should convey them to their master, for which they were to receive twenty shillings, and sixpence for each mile. Or, if the master were not known, then the servant should be conveyed to the common jail in Charles Town, the jailer being obligated, under penalty of forty shillings, to make the above payments.[17] The marshal was to keep such servants in custody till they should be claimed. Then he should deliver them, on payment of the charges he had been under, including payments made for delivery at the jail, cost of diet during the period of custody, and 2s.6d. for every twenty-four hours of such custody. If such a prisoner escaped, the marshal was liable to the master in the amount allowed by a jury at common law.[18]

In 1744 provision was made for whipping escaped servants through the parish, after proof had been made before a justice of the peace that they were fugitives. This duty was passed on from constable to constable through all intervening parishes, till the Charleston jail was reached. The warden was obliged to advertise such prisoners in the *Gazette*, and keep them at hard labor for thirty days. If the prisoner was not redeemed, or could not prove himself a free man, within the space of three weeks, he should "be whipped on the bare back, not exceeding twenty lashes, and be turned out of the said workhouse." [19] According to the law of 1744, any servant found more than two miles from home should be deemed a fugitive unless he could show written permission from his master, mistress, or overseer.[20]

While severe punishments were provided for certain offenses, the penalty of added service was the most usual form, though supplemented by corporal punishment. The case of John Radcliffe was an early example of the former. A contemporary, Dennis Mahoon, was sentenced to "be stripped naked to his Waste & receive thirty nine lashes upon his naked back." [21] This was his punishment for a second offense in persuading fellow servants to run away with him to the Spaniards. Likewise, Philip Orrill received twenty-one lashes for "refusing to observe his [mistress's] lawful commands and more especially . . . for threatning to oversett the Boate wherein she was or words to that effect, and giving the provisions allowed to him . . . to the Doggs and threatning to runn away to the Indians, and divers other Gross abuses and destructive practices."[22] Both these cases were in the early period.

Decided differentiation is apparent in the provisions for punishment of servants and of slaves. Slaves and Indians convicted of boat stealing were to receive thirty-nine lashes for the first offense, and have one ear cut off for the second.[23] A white servant "shall be liable to the same penalties and punishments as any white free person". Then if his master did not pay the fine imposed, he might be sold for not exceeding four years.

The Act of 1717 provided "that in all cases where a freeman is punishable by fines,[24] . . . a servant shall receive corporal punishment, for every twenty shillings fine, nine lashes, and so many such several punishments as there is twenty shillings included in the fine, unless the master or other acquaintance shall redeem them by making payment."[25] The Act of 1744 adds: "provided the whole doth not exceed thirty-nine lashes."[26] A servant getting a woman servant with child must serve her master to make up for her service lost. For marriage between servants, without the master's consent, the penalty was a year of added service by the man, or payment of a fine of twenty pounds.[27] The penalty for men or women involved in mésalliances with Negroes was seven years additional service.[28]

Except for the fact that some thirty-seven years elapsed between the two sentences, there appears a good comparison between the punishment meted out to a white woman servant in 1717 and that for a Negro woman slave in 1754, both of whom had been found guilty of arson. Ann Tuffen, whose record for burning buildings had followed her from England to South Carolina, was ordered purchased from her master and deported to the Bahamas.[29] The issue of this sentence is not definitely reported. Governor Daniell advised the House, six months after the case was first decided, that he knew not "by what intercession, that hath been offered in her behalf, she is not yet sent off."[30] On the same day, the House returned answer that their former message "was very particular as to the case of the said Ann Tuffen; and the Public Receiver is hereby ordered to pay for her out of the Public Treasury."[31] Whether Ann left the country or not does not appear. Perhaps this is just as well, since the case of Sachavisa, the Negro woman, is also doubtful as to the issue of the sentence passed. Statement of this latter case appears in an order by Governor Glen "to all and Singular our

Judges, Justices, Constables and other our Ministers . . . Whereas Sachavisa, a Negro Woman Slave . . . has been accused of Willfully burning the Dwelling House of . . . Childermas Croft [her master] and was thereupon Capitally convicted and Sentence passed upon the Said Sachavisa that her Body Should be burned; Now Know Ye that wee being Piously minded have respited the Execution of the Said Sentence for the Space of one week. . . ."[32]

In 1712, petty larceny by slaves was punishable by no more than 40 lashes for the first offense, cutting off one ear or branding in the forehead for the second, slitting the nose for the third, and death, at the option of the judges, for the fourth.[33] Evidence of the execution of such sentences is wanting, except as claims appear for Negroes who have been executed.[34] Even here, it is not shown that such capital punishment was visited upon them for any other than very heinous offences. Some of the advertisers in the *Gazette* were quite bloody-minded, if we are to believe all they say about their runaway slaves.

One such, in 1745, says he is "willing to allow any man that will bring him Toney's head the sum of ten pounds."[35] Patrick Laird, fourteen years later, gives notice that if his "negro wench, named *Nell* . . . shall enter my service before Thursday the 5th of next month, she shall be well used; but if she does not come in to me by that time, I offer FIVE POUNDS to any person that shall deliver her to me alive, and TWENTY POUNDS for her head."[36] The House put itself on record, to a like effect, when it ordered a bill brought in providing "that an Encouragement be given for bringing in the Scalps of such Men or Women Negro Slaves that are already deserted or shall hereafter desert who shall be found beyond Savanna River and cannot be taken & brought home alive to wit, for each Scalp with the two Ears £20. to be paid out of the Public Treasury."[37]

While his Negro blood identified the slave,[38] thus making it a comparatively easy matter to keep track of him, much difficulty was experienced with white servants. The servant out of his time could demand his certificate of freedom which would act as a pass and safeguard for him. But the presumption that a strange white was a runaway servant could not always have been a safe one to act upon. Many times a servant would be "entertained" unawares. Still oftener would he be taken in by those who knew his identity but, for reasons of their own, were interested in helping him.

The "entertaining" of servants and trading with them appear as the two great evils difficult to guard against. Section VI of the Act of 1717 reads: "And whereas divers ill-disposed persons do secretly and covertly truck and trade with other men's servants and apprentices, who to the great injury of their masters are thereby induced and encouraged to steal, purloin and embessel their master's goods; Be it therefore enacted, That what person or persons soever, shall buy, sell, trade or barter with any servant for any commodity whatsoever, without lycense or consent of such servant's master or mistress, he or they so offending against the premises, shall forfeit to the master or mistress of such servants, treble the value of things traded for, bought or sold, and also ten pound current money to him that shall inform for the same. . . ." [39] This amount must be sued for within twenty-five days "by action of debt in any court of record."[40]

The "entertaining" evil had two aspects. First, as has been noted, was the entertaining or harboring of fugitive servants, which was dealt with under the laws for runaways. Those who should "entertain or harbour any servant running away from his master's service, and not having a certificate . . . shall pay to the master of such servant for every day and night two pounds current money, for all the time he shall harbour or entertain him, so that the whole exceed not treble the value of the servant's remaining time to be served with the master or mistress." [41] Section XIV of the Act of 1717 provides "That if any punch-house keeper, vintner or other person whatsoever, shall entertain any man's servant any time, if the said servant shall be drunk, trade or game during such time, he or they so offending shall forfeit forty shillings. . . ." [42] Thomas Monck gives notice, in the *Gazette* of March and April, 1734, "to caution all private Persons as well as Publick-House Keepers, against entertaining . . . *Thomas Bond* on any Pretence or Excuse whatsoever, otherwise they will be prosecuted with the utmost severity of the Law." [43]

Even more explicit is the following: "Whereas *Mr. Blondel, George Wyss,* Mr. *Morphew* in Broad street and others keep and entertain Negroes and Servants, at their Masters great damage, and whereas *Wm. Matthews, Frank Glin,* Servants, and *William Watkins* Apprentice to Hugh Evans, Taylor in *Charlestown,* have absented themselves several times from their Masters Service: This is therefore to forwarn every Person, not to keep or entertain the said Servants and Apprentice, or either of them, in any publick or private House by day or by night, without their having their Masters Leave, or else they may expect to be sued after this warning according to Law." [44]

However, while the numerous Acts for the better regulating of white servants were principally in the nature of restrictions upon their liberty, the welfare of the servant and his or her rights were by no means overlooked. For example, take the striking of a master by the servant and the punishment of the servant by his master. For the former offense, a servant might be sentenced to serve an added period, not exceeding six months, or receive corporal punishment not exceeding twenty-one stripes. [45] Yet even as early as 1691, "if any master or mistress or overseer shall under pretext of correction whipp and unreasonably abuse his, her or their servant or servants, such servant or servants complaining to the Grand Councill and makeing good his said complaint by good proofe, of which the Grand Councill are judges, then it may bee and shall bee lawful for the said Grand Councill to sett such servant or servants at their liberty, or to make such other order or orders for the relief of the servant or servants as in their wisdom shall bee thought most just." [46]

Such cases were of not infrequent occurrence. Following the complaint of Elizabeth Jones against her master, John Raven, the former was ordered to "Returne to and Continue with her Said Master and behave her Selfe," and that Raven find her "Sufficient Cloatthing, meatt and drinck and moderatt Correction onely Either by himselfe or others and farther that the Said Raven doe use the best of his Indeavours to teach the Said Jones what he is obliged to doe by the Said Indentures." [47]

The same remedy is provided by the same Act of 1691 "if any master or mistresse or overseer shall refuse to give or allowe his or their servant or servants good wholesome and sufficient meate, drinke and lodging and apparell." John Maverick was financially embarrassed to the extent that he was unable to supply his servant, Christopher Field, with necessary provisions and clothing. So the Grand Council authorized Captain Florence O'Sullivan to provide for the said Field until the gathering of the next crop. [48] Richard Nicklin complained that he was not freed from his indentures, although he had served the two years for which he had agreed. He was ordered to serve another year; and if he could prove his statements in that time, he was to have "sufficient satisfaccon for the third yeares service." [49] Richard Sims, a servant, by "Daniel Bullman Attorney" sued his master, John Evans. The dispute was concerning certain absence of the servant and a discrepancy in accounts, the servant having acted as agent for the master. After a hearing, the matter was left "to theire farther Remedy att Law when the Said Sims shall appear in person and all Costs of Suites to be equally paid between them." [50]

The Grand Council could not long be troubled with the oversight of all these details, and later Laws provided that the Justices of the Peace look after servant questions. The Act of 1744, still the guide at the close of the colonial period, made like provisions with those above-mentioned; and, in addition, provided a series of definite penalties. ". . . if the said justice shall find by lawful proof that the said servant's complaint is just, he was impowered and required, under the penalty of Five Pounds proclamation-money, by warrant under his hand and seal directed to the next constable to levy and distrain the goods and chattels of such master or mistress, any sum not exceeding Four Pounds proclamation-money, to be disposed of for the use of the poor of the parish where such offence is committed. And for the second offence, any two justices of the peace are authorized and required . . . to make an order directed to any constable to sell and dispose of the remaining time of service of such servant to any other white person, for such money as can be got for the same, to be paid to the church wardens of the parish where the offence is committed, for the use of the poor." [51] Provision is made, further, for appeal to the Governor and Council. Laurens' letter, quoted above, is evidence of the readiness of servants late in the colonial period to take advantage of such provisions. Sick servants were to be properly cared for. Besides the equipment to be furnished at the end of the term, definite proof of the completion of service had to be given.

CHAPTER VIII

Life of the Servant

LEGISLATION APPLICABLE to white servants furnishes a substantial guide to the determination of their social status, but however harsh the treatment actually accorded this lower stratum, it was usually in advance of the statutory provisions for their regulation and punishment. This was true in England itself till well into the nineteenth century. The laws, as they appear at any given time, are apt to suggest a more desperate condition than actually existed. Yet those of South Carolina reflect a decided public interest in the welfare of the white servant class.

Discussion of the legislation bearing immediately upon this element of population has brought out the fact that while their liberty was circumscribed, the conditions under which they served were not especially onerous. In fact, they were doubtless often an improvement over those under which free inhabitants of the same classes lived in their native countries.[1] Moreover, not only was provision made for the legal safeguarding of the rights of the servant, but evidence is not wanting to prove that the protection of the law was actually accorded them. This refers only to their legal rights. Consideration must also be given the kind of treatment accorded them by their masters and mistresses.

Turning again, for comparative discussion, to Barbados, Governor Atkins in 1680 wrote the Lords of Trade and Plantations: "It is forbidden under a considerable penalty of sugar to bury any Christian servant until so many freeholders of the neighborhood have viewed the corpse to make sure that he may not have met a violent death at the hands of his master." [2] This is contemporary with the cases cited where servants in Carolina were suing at law because of failure of their masters to accord them the treatment they were entitled to.[3] At the period when the use of white servants was at its height in South Carolina, the public attitude toward their treatment was fairly reflected in the report of the committee appointed to investigate the treatment of prisoners in jail at Charleston. This committee reported that the prisoners were not getting the stipulated "one Pound of Beef and one Pound of Bread," for which the provost marshal was given a daily allowance of six shillings and three pence per prisoner. A further recommendation was made to the effect that proper clothing and medical attention be given a man, committed for felony, who was in need of better care.[4]

Such an attitude toward a malefactor makes safe the conjecture that the actual treatment of white servants was commensurate with the legal provisions for their well-being. The only specific reference to cruelty comparable with that exercised in the other colonies is found in a letter from Henry Laurens. But it should be noted that he is making charges, not against masters of servants in the colony, but against the ships' captains who were bringing them in. He says he "never saw an Instance of Cruelty in Ten or Twelve years experience in that branch [referring to the African trade] equal to the cruelty exercised upon those poor Irish. . . . Self-Interest prompted the baptized Heathen [captains] to take some care of their wretched Slaves for a Market, but no other care was taken of those poor Protestant Christians from Ireland but to deliver as many as possible alive on Shoar upon the cheapest Terms."[5]

Referring to Virginia experience, a letter to the Council of Trade and Plantations of June 8th, 1702, described an ingenious plan for the evasion of responsibility for "supplying" servants at the end of their time. "A man had really better be hanged than come a servant into the Plantations, most of his food being homene and water, which is good for negroes, but very disagreeable to English constitutions. I have been told by some of them that they have not tasted fresh meat once in three months. When their time is expired, according to custom they are to have a certain allowance of corn and clothes, which in Maryland I think is to the value of £6., but in Virginia not so much, to save which a Planter about three months before the expiration of a servant's time will use him barbarously, and to gain a month's freedome the poor servant gladly quits his pretensions to that allowance, which drives a great many of them into Proprietary Governments, where their labour is of little benefit to the Crown."[6]

Servant and master were often quite close. In many cases, an added bounty or an early release is indicative of this. The special opportunity for such award offered itself when the master or mistress died before the expiration of the servant's time. Thus, Francis Le Brasseur bequeathed to his "White Servant boy named Jacob Marki, Fifteen pounds Current money of South Carolina yearly . . . during the time of his Servitude." Further, the executors of the estate are directed to "put the said boy to School to be taught reading and writing." [7] William Rose bequeathed to his "Beloved friend Caterenor Munsey her indentors of Servitude for Three Years which She has still to serve." [8] Jacob Roth's will provides "Thirdly, . . . unto my Servant Girl Annah Apleonya, a Cow and Calf or a Mare and Colt which she pleaseth to have and her Freedom if my Wife should die before her time is out." [9]

Alexander Vander Dussen was still more liberal, leaving his servant Charles Murrine £1000 currency, and a like amount to Anne Killpatrick "to be put out at interest for her use till she shall Arrive at the Years of Twenty one or marriage, the Interest to go in the mean time for her Maintenance and when she arrives at the aforesaid years of Twenty one or marriage then the Principal to be paid to her." [10] An interesting bequest of slaves to a servant appears in the will of John Summers, under the date of January 4, 1743, "I will and Bequeath to my Maid Sarah one negro Woman Jeny and to each of her Children a negro and all the rest of my Estate both Real and personal, I will and Bequeath to the said Sarah and her Children." [11]

The colorful nature of servant life is nowhere better illustrated than in the pages of the South Carolina *Gazette*. The trades at which men worked, the clothes they wore, personal peculiarities they developed, the comparative value of their services, the mixture of population which facilitated escape from service all appear in frequent advertisements for runaways.

In the *Gazette* of February 19, 1732, appears the following notice, which is fairly typical of all runaway advertisements: "Run away from his Master *John Fisher*, at Will Town, a white Servant, named Caleb Lowle, aged about 18, by Trade a Taylor, having on a red Whitney Coat: He is a slim Lad, with a round pale Face. Whoever will give Notice of the said Servant, so as he may be had again, or if taken, will send him to Charles-Town Goal, shall have £10. Reward, and all Charges paid." [12] While these notices are but briefly descriptive, from the whole number of such may be gathered a considerable fund of information on such points as trades, nationality, wearing apparel, and oftentimes the thread of a personal history, which it would be most interesting to follow if that were possible. Thus, "Joseph Dopson, Taylor in Middle street" offers £10. for the return of Richard Riches, who has run away with Isabelle Shaw; the latter described as "of middle size, well set, round visage and a likely face." [13]

John Whatnell is advertised for, being described as "a middle sized man, fair complexion, tender-eyed, pretty well set, full fac'd, quick spoken, and had on when he went away a yellow orange colour'd Coat, coarse cloath, trimm'd with black, Ozenbrig Trowsers, Dimitty Jacket, and a white Garlix Shirt." [14] Jonathan Lewellen prepared for the future when he absented himself, for "he had with him when he went away 3 Coats. 2 Shirts, one pair Oznabrigs & one pair of Leather Breeches, 2 pair of Stockings, 1 pair of Pumps, & 1 pair of Shoes." [15] Peter Lister "got a pass from Justice Young by his cunning; he has enticed an Angola Negro to go along with him." [16] Throughout July, August, and September 1751, Peter Timothy, publisher of the *Gazette*, advertised for his Irish printer, Robert Whitaker. Evidently Robert was returned and received an added term of service for, six years later, his master was again advertising for him.[17]

Mr. John Page, of Pon Pon, advertised in June and July of 1742 for "an indented likely young Welch Woman, named Ruth Willcock." Either she was returned and again absented herself, or her master grew exasperated at her continued absence for, by September of the same year, she had become "a thick squat Welch Servant Woman." [18] Mr. Page might, perhaps have displayed greater wisdom by using his personal descriptions in reverse order.

When the poor Protestants entered indenture as families, [19] they were found running away, also in families. William Thompson, who "used to wear a blue Frock with green Sleeves, and his own black Hair," his wife, who "Stoops in her shoulders and has a very wrinkled Face," and "Her Daughter . . . about 14 Years of Age, fair Hair'd and slender" deserted in a canoe with three other men, from Captain Mark Carr, in Georgia.[20] And John Paul Traut and his wife, Anna, both German, took 'French leave' of Patrick Hinds.[21] Stranger still than this Irish master of a German family is

Moses Cohin's advertisement for his runaway "Dutch servant girl." [22] Among the high-priced servants advertised for are James Hewitt, "formerly a Schoolmaster in New England,[23] and Richard Aalder, a Dutch barkeeper. For the return of the latter to "the Three Legs of a Man in King Street," a reward of £50 is offered.[24] The school-master was, of course, worth less, by £20, in terms of the reward offered.[25]

Such a one as the peruke-maker who went away in "a light-coloured Coat, with a red Plush Cape, Linnen-Jacket, fine Shirt, Blue Cloth Breeches, white Stockings, and a pair of good Pump Shoes" [26] would have been the proper subject for this witticism had he run away fourteen years earlier:

"A Hue and Cry, after an Irish Dear Joy.
"Cito Ignominia fit, superbi gloria
"Mendax Calumnia vitam Corrumpit..
"An Irish Mungrel, lately Run away,
When *R—ge* thought to shew him English play,
But *Teague,* it seems, did not think fit to stay.
Awake my Muse, in lively Colours paint
A D—l incarnate though he's call'd a *Saint,*
A batter'd Beau, puff'd up with haughty pride,
Full of himself, scorns all the World beside,
A hare-brain'd Fop, impertinent and odd,
Whose heaven's his belly, and whose back's his God,
A Great conceited Fop, without pretence
To the least grain of Learning, Wit or Sense
Or any thing but Irish Impudence;—" [27]

A most fascinating story of a servant is that of Sarah Wilson, alias Princess Susanna Carolina Matilda, as reported in the *London Magazine.*

Some time ago one Sarah Wilson, who attended upon Miss Vernon, sister to Lady Grosvenor, and maid of honour to the queen, having found means to be admitted into one of the royal apartments, took occasion to break open a cabinet, and rifled it of many valuable jewels, for which she was apprehended, tried, and condemned to die; but through the interposition of her mistress, her sentence was softened into transportation.

Accordingly, in the fall of 1771, she was landed in Maryland, where she was exposed to sale and purchased. After a short residence in that place, she very secretly decamped, and escaped into Virginia, travelled through that colony and through North to South Carolina. When at a proper distance from her purchaser, she assumed the title of the Princess Susanna Carolina Mitalda, pronouncing herself to be an own sister to our sovereign lady the queen. She had carried with her her clothes that served to favour the deception, and had secured a part of the jewels together with Her Majesty's picture.

She travelled from one gentleman's house to another under these pretensions, making astonishing impressions in many places, affecting the mode of royalty so inimitably that many had the honour to kiss her hand. To some she promised governments, to others regiments, with promotions of all kinds in the treasury, army, and the royal navy. In short, she acted her part so plausibly as to persuade the generality that she was no impostor. In vain did many sensible gentlemen in those parts exert themselves to detect and make a proper example of her; for she had levied heavy contributions upon some persons of the highest rank in the southern colonies.

At length, however, an advertisement appeared, and a messenger arrived from her master, who raised a loud hue and cry for her serene highness. The lady was then on an excursion of a few miles to a neighboring plantation, for which the messenger had set out when the gentleman who had brought this information left Charles-town (Charleston).[28]

CHAPTER IX

The Servant Out of His Time

IT IS SCARCELY FAIR TO THIS DISCUSSION to drop the white servant as soon as he is "out of his time." His importance lay not only in the service rendered while under indenture or serving his time for payment of his passage, but even more in the contribution he would make as a future citizen. It is necessary therefore to follow him beyond his servant days.

There were two places for the servant to go when "out of his time." He might remain in Charles Town or move to the back country. Charles Town, perhaps of all colonial cities, was constituted of regularly graded social strata of somewhat equal proportions. It claimed the most exclusive aristocracy attended by a great entourage of Negro slaves. Between these two extremes many gradations existed. There were the importing merchants of wealth and position, small shop-keepers and tradesmen, artisans both free and indentured, and, as time went on, hired employees more nearly approaching the status of present day labor. Within this stratified society there was, however, mobility.

The white servant in Charles Town, when "out of his time," might simply hang out his own shingle. Abraham Daphne, carpenter, gave public notice that "being now acquitted and discharged from all engagements with *Humphrey Sommers,*" he was ready "to undertake any work in his business, at reasonable prices. . . . He may be spoke with at Mr. *John Ballantine's* at *White Point,* or Mr. *Goltier's* in *King Street.*" [1] This sort of graduation from service into independent business had been going on for some time, as the *Gazette* showed an increasing number of such cards. There were announcements of bricklayers, carpenters, coopers, goldsmiths, gunsmiths and blacksmiths, joiners, sailmakers, staymakers, shoemakers, tailors, tinners, watchmakers and clockmakers.

By mid-century there began to appear "situation-wanted" and "help-wanted" cards. "A young man lately arrived from England wants a place as bookkeeper or accountant." [2] A Young woman, who has served her time in a family with fidelity, and can be well recommended, wants a place."[3] "A young woman of unexceptionable character" advertised: "Wants a place as Housekeeper in any respectable family in town." [4] "A Gardener, Wants employment." [5]

In the "help-wanted" columns there were such advertisements as: "A Young Lady going to Virginia by Sea . . . is desirous of carrying with her a sober, discreet Person of her own Sex, either in the Capacity of a Companion or waiting woman." [6] In 1772: "Wanted to Hire . . . a good plain Cook, either Man or Woman, to live in Charles Town; good Wages will be given, an easy Place, and good Usage." [7] These all have a modern ring. However, it is not always clear whether or not there is still an indenture in the background. The following is an example: "A Handy, active, honest, healthy waiting man, about Seventeen Years of Age, who can shave, and is well acquainted with the Management of Horses, to be hired out by the Month. . . . T. Powell & Co." [8]

The settling of large numbers of artisans in Charles Town, the major city of the southern colonies, eventually resulted in a considerable middle class. These artisans, some of whom had been indentured servants, were those who had moved up the social ladder. There was the possibility that an indentured servant once freed might make his way to the top of society, becoming eventually a planter. None has actually been traced. However, the greatest of the mechanics certainly did end their careers as members of the aristocracy. Daniel Cannon, carpenter, owned a plantation just out of town. John Paul Grimké, silversmith, owned 500 acres of Edisto Island. Jonathan Sarazin, silversmith, bought 1,296 acres in St. John's parish, and became a rice planter.[9] The lines between the classes were certainly blurred in this fluid American society.

A glance at the geological map of South Carolina shows three main divisions, running generally from northeast to southwest, roughly paralleling the coast: the low country, the middle country, and the back country. Frederick Law Olmsted, who visited the state in the mid-nineteenth century, has left a graphic description of the low country. He wrote: "A large part of all the country next the coast, fifty miles or more in width . . . is occupied by flat cypress swamps and reedy marshes. . . . At distant intervals there are shallow breaches through which the quiet tide twice a day steals in, swelling the neutral lagoons and damming the outlet of the fresh water streams, till their current is destroyed or turned back, and their flood dispersed far and wide over the debatable land of the cypress swamps. Then when the heavy rains in the interior have swollen the rivers, their eddying currents deposit, all along the edges of the sandy islands and capes of the swamps, the rich freight they have brought from the calcareous or granitic mountains in which they rise, with the organic waste of the great forests through which they flow. With all is mingled the silicious wash of the nearest shore and the rich silt of the salt lagoons aroused from their bottoms in extraordinary assaults of the ocean. This is the soil of the rice plantations." [10]

This was the choicest land in the colony and had been granted early to the proprietors and their friends. Thus Ashley Barony, on the south side of the Ashley River, was granted in 1675 to Lord Ashley. Fairlawn, on the west side of the Cooper River, was granted in 1678 to Peter Colleton. Cypress, at the head of the east branch of the Cooper, went in 1683 to Thomas Colleton. In the same year, Wadboo, at the head of the west branch of the Cooper, was given to James Colleton. In 1709 Seewee, on the north side of Bull's Bay, went to Sir Nathaniel Johnson. In 1711, Winyah, on the south side of Winyah Bay, was granted to Robert Daniel. In 1718, Hobcaw, at the mouth of the Waccamaw River, was assigned to Lord John Carteret. Raphoe, on the south side of the Santee, was laid out for Landgrave John Bayley.[11] The low country had in this fashion been carved up for the great men. The servant who desired land had to go beyond the coastal fringe, so if he did not go to Charles Town he would go to the back country.

Those who had been white servants on the plantations would certainly have looked to the back country for land of their own. The required equipment at the end of service, as noted in the indentures of the early period, was for planting. The desire to come to America was a desire for independent status. An indenture status was, after all, only a temporary interruption in this desire. These people and their descendants would find their opportunities in the country. The back country of South Carolina, with the neighboring frontier of Georgia, constituted the focal point for this migration.

In the back country these people met another group coming down from the north, many of whom were servants just freed or sons of servants. "The largest bodies of the Germans and Scotch-Irish who settled the piedmont and mountainous regions from Maryland to Georgia came to America through the ports of Philadelphia and Newcastle, Delaware, and finding lands occupied in Pennsylvania and New Jersey were gradually pushed toward the south, till they were met by a smaller stream of the same people who came through the port of Charleston to South Carolina and thence to the frontier." [12]

Throughout the second and third quarters of the eighteenth century ever increasing numbers came to settle the upcountry and the backcountry. Meriwether has written: "The back country was separated from the tidewater and its well established institutions by the wide and thinly settled middle country, and by other barriers even more serious. Indeed, many of its interests and connections drew it to the piedmont settlements of the colonies to the north. . . ." [13] Germans and Scotch-Irish had constituted the dominant factors in the settlement of western Pennsylvania. Faust,[14] Hanna,[15] and Ford [16] have demonstrated the importance of these elements in the population throughout the length of the Allegheny valleys. While the greater part of these settlers came down from the Pennsylvania backcountry, there were numbers also from western Virginia and North Carolina. It is not too much to assume that many of them had begun their American experience as servants; and if such would make the long trek from the north, assuredly the same thing happened to others who started in South Carolina.

The author of the *Treatise on Georgia* gave what is a very excellent summary of the upcountry labor problem and suggested, at the same time, something of a prophecy in its bearing on the future of these poor but deserving immigrants. "It must be . . . [confessed], that divers of these Foreigners have, during the Time of their Servitude, shewn themselves of a dogged Disposition, surly and obstinate, discovering an Averseness to their Masters Orders, which proceeds (as we imagine) from a Dislike of their being subject to Strangers; whilst others again have behaved well; but it may be alledged with Truth, that when or wheresoever among us, any of them have worked for their own Benefit, they are indefatigable, and outdone by none, which joined with great Parsimony, fits them for excellent Settlers when free." [17]

Shortly before the Revolution, an admiring diarist, referring to Charleston, wrote that, "Its citizens . . . so rich . . . so luxurious, so polite a people owed their privileges to rice, indigo, slavery, law and trade." But the best he could say of backcountry folks was that occasionally one might find some single person who "is decent." Also he found the tide-water and the frontier in a state of chronic political feuding for "though the Back Country fills fast with new Settlers, yet our Assembly will not lay out new parishes, lest by increasing the Number of Assembly Men, they lessen Town Interest, which is opposite to the Country. . . . Even settlers who knew their parish, could not vote without a long trip to the parish churches near the coast, where ballotting took place." [18]

Dr. Schaper, in the introduction to his *Sectionalism in South Carolina* states that "Her peculiar economic system and her peculiar social structure have given rise to many difficult political and constitutional problems . . . the contour and extent of the land, the position of mountain ranges, the soil, temperature, rainfall, navigable waters, good harbors, waterfalls, mineral deposits, forests, fish, and game . . . were . . . conditions which, with the Indian social system, combined to produce the American environment.

"The second factor was the people themselves—the customs, laws, languages, and institutions which they brought with them. . . ."[19] The spectacle of two types of society—one based on slave labor, the other resting essentially on free labor—existing side by side under the same Government, we can observe in the early history of South Carolina." [20]

At the close of the eighteenth century, two-thirds of the slaves and seven-ninths of the wealth were possessed by one-fifth of the population in the low country.[21] The apportionment of representation in the State legislature in 1790 was based on 28,644 whites and 79,216 colored for the tide-water. For the upcountry there were 111,534 whites and 29,679 colored. The low country had 20 senators and 70 representatives; the upcountry, 17 senators and 54 representatives.[22] "The whole struggle," according to Schaper, had "centered about the apportionment of representation in the State legislature." [23]

On the basis of these facts, the contrast between the people of the two sections becomes distinct. Applying these observations to the larger field of our national history, two reasonable inferences may be noted. First, the white servant element was an outstanding factor in the settlement of the backcountry, where their descendants became an important part of the political opposition to the low country aristocracy. Secondly, while the artisan class in Charles Town, recruited largely from white servants, constituted a most important factor in the city's growth and prominence, their position was so far inferior as to germinate the seeds of a like opposition here in aristocracy's stronghold.

Ulrich B. Phillips took about the same stand. Writing on "The South Carolina Federalists," he states: "In the internal politics of South Carolina, an aristocracy composed of the planters and the leading Charleston merchants was generally in control of the state government, but was in chronic dread of defeat at the ballot-boxes. In opposition there was a body of clerks, artisans and other white laborers in Charleston, much inclined at times to assert democratic doctrine, and there was a large population of farmers in the distant uplands, non-slave-holding in the eighteenth century, disposed to co-operate with the submerged Charleston democracy on occasion. . . ." [24]

The white servants played a twofold part in the history of the colony of South Carolina: one part was economic, the other political. They played the part of skilled laborers in town and on the plantations until they had worked out their time. After that they became men of free and independent status and as such lent their strength to the growth of democracy both in town and country. The fact that they did not constitute a major labor force in agriculture, as they did in Virginia, does not mean that they were of no importance in Carolina. Nor does the fact that they were far fewer in number than in the colonies to the north mean that they were a negligible quantity in the history of the province and state. Gradually, over the years, their influence was felt in the rugged individualism that helped to make for a balance of power in the affairs of state.

NOTES FOR THE INTRODUCTION

[1] James Curtis Ballagh, "White Servitude in the Colony of Virginia," *Johns Hopkins University Studies in Historical and Political Science*, XIII (1895).

[2] John Spencer Bassett, "Slavery and Servitude in the Colony of North Carolina," *ibid.*, XIV (1896).

[3] Karl F. Geiser, "Redemptioners and Indentured Servants in the Colony and Commonwealth of Pennsylvania," Supplement to *Yale Review* (1901).

[4] Eugene Irving McCormac, "White Servitude in Maryland, 1634-1820," *Johns Hopkins University Studies in Historical and Political Science*, XXII (1904).

[5] Ballagh, *op. cit.*, p. 352.

[6] Bassett, *op. cit.*, p. 183.

[7] *The American Historical Review*, X (1904-05), 212.

[8] A. Maurice Low, *The American People, A Study in National Psychology* (Boston: Houghton Mifflin Company, 1911), I, 323-324.

[9] Theo. D. Jervey, "The White Indented Servants of South Carolina," *The South Carolina Historical and Genealogical Magazine*, XII (1911), 167.

[10] Elizabeth Donnan, "The Slave Trade into South Carolina Before the Revolution," *The American Historical Review*, XXXIII (1927-28), 804-805.

[11] Arthur Henry Hirsch, *The Huguenots of Colonial South Carolina* (Durham: Duke University Press, 1928), p. 179.

[12] Robert L. Meriwether, *The Expansion of South Carolina, 1729-1765* (Kingsport: Southern Publishers, Inc., 1940), p. 17.

[13] Abbot Emerson Smith, *Colonists in Bondage* (Chapel Hill: The University of North Carolina Press, 1947), p. 33.

CHAPTER I

[1] John Esten Cooke, *Virginia, A History of the People* (Boston: Houghton Mifflin Company, 1887), p. 367.

[2] *See* statement of Governor Sir Jonathan Atkins of Barbados that "three blacks work better and cheaper than one white man." *CSP, Colonial*, IX, 1022.

[3] Governor Atkins reported 2,193 white servants and 37,315 Negroes in 1680. *Ibid.*, X, 1336.

Whites had been field hands. One man had inspected many plantations "and seen 30 or 40 English, Scotch and Irish at work in the parching sun, without shirt, shoe or stocking." *Ibid.*, V, 1657.

Lord Culpeper reported from Virginia in 1681 that there were 15,000 servants and 3,000 blacks in a population of 70 to 80,000. *Ibid.*, XI, 320.

[4] *Ibid.*, V, 528.

[5] *Ibid.*, I, 421.

[6] *Ibid.*, I, 427.

[7] *Ibid.*

[8] *Ibid.*, V, 175.

[9] *Ibid.*, I, 367; V, 1565 and 1727; VII, 1116; XIII, 2449; XVI, 272. *See also* the acts to encourage: *Ibid.*, X, 609; XI, 583 and 1919; XV, 192.

10 Edward McCrady, *The History of South Carolina under the Proprietary Government, 1670-1719* (New York: The Macmillan Company, 1897), p. 121, n. 1. The *number* of servants with each free passenger agrees with the statement in *CSP, Colonial*, VII, 97-i.

11 *Ibid.*, VII, 33(86). *Also see* W. Roy Smith, *South Carolina as a Royal Province, 1719-1776* (New York: The Macmillan Company, 1903), p. 27.

12 Fragmentary volume MS Records of the Secretary of the Province, p. 13.

13 *Ibid.*, p. 6.

14 *Journal of Grand Council, 1671-1680*, pp. 22-3, 50.

15 *See* "Fundamental Constitutions" in B. R. Carroll, *Historical Collections of South Carolina* (New York, 1836), II, 363.

16 *CSP, Colonial*, VII, 515.

17 *Ibid.*, IX, 944.

18 *Ibid.*, IX, 590.

19 *Ibid.*, XI, 541.

20 *Ibid.*, XI, 1017. Also *LT*, No. 1, p. 238.

21 *CSP, Colonial*, XI, 1905.

22 W. Roy Smith, *op. cit.*, p. 27.

23 *CSP, Colonial*, X, 992. A copy of the same instructions can be found in *LT*, No. 1, pp. 82-83.

24 *Ibid.*, p. 149.

25 *Ibid.*

26 *Ibid.*, pp. 149-50.

27 *CSP, Colonial*, XII, 639.

28 *Ibid.*, XII, 1962.

29 *LT*, III, 58; and *Warrants for Land Grants (1692-1711)*, p. 54.

30 *Secretary's Records Commissions and Instructions (1685-1712)*, p. 199.

31 *CSP, Colonial*, XVIII, 470.

32 Ratified October 8, 1698. *Trott MS*, p. 153. Same in *JCHA*, I, 193-206.

33 *Trott MS*, p. 663. Also *JCHA*, V, 62, 89, 91, 101, 104, 126, 132, and 135.

34 *Warrants to Land Grants (1692-1711)*, p. 66.

35 *Ibid.*, p. 54.

36 Carroll, *op. cit.*, II, 125.

CHAPTER II

1 *See* Chapter I, n. 13.

2 *Gazette*, March 2, 1747.

3 *PCR (1736-1739)*, pp. 299-300.

4 *Gazette*, September 25-October 2, 9-16, 16-23, 1736.

5 *Ibid.*, September 13, 1751.

6 *Ibid.*, July 20, 1734.

7 *Ibid.*, October 12, 1734.

8 *Ibid.*, January 19, 1738.

9 *Ibid.*, October 1, 1744.

10 *Ibid.*, May 28, 1750.

11 *Ibid.*, May 31, 1740.

12 *Ibid.*, March 5, 1737.

¹³ *Ibid.,* January 20-27, 1733.

¹⁴ *Letter Books of Henry Laurens, Merchant (1762-1764),* p. 200.

CHAPTER III

¹ *CSP, Colonial,* XI, 540.

² *JCHA,* I, 233.

³ *Trott MS,* pp. 217-18.

⁴ At the close of the war of the Austrian Succession there was an attempt to colonize 4,000 discharged troops in Nova Scotia. There were similar suggestions made for New York, Virginia, Maryland, and Barbados. *CSP, Colonial,* XV, 1407 and 1412; XVI, 5.

⁵ *LT,* VI, 163.

⁶ *JCHA,* V, 153.

⁷ *Trott MS,* p. 666. *See also JCHA,* V, 158. Four years later, the Assembly requested the Governor to assure these men "that they shall, if they continue where they now be, after the said time in the Public service, they shall from that time be allowed the same pay as other Public soldiers . . . ." *Ibid.,* 457.

⁸ *Ibid.,* VII, 376.

⁹ *Ibid.,* XIV, 166.

¹⁰ *Ibid.,* XI, 5-27.

¹¹ *Ibid.,* VII, 456.

¹² *Ibid.,* III, 552.

¹³ Act No. 314 in *Trott MS,* "The Laws of the Province of South Carolina," p. 480.

¹⁴ *JCHA,* V, 119.

¹⁵ In June 1714 the Governor and Council had recommended a Bill "allowing a premium of four or five pounds per head to any person who shall import white servants into this Province, which we are of opinion will be a greater encouragement for the bringing of white people into this Province than anything that hath hitherto been thought of." *Ibid.,* IV, 269.

Contrary to the opinion of the House, the Council continued to urge this plan in 1716. Possibly they figured the obligation of the new Bill (requiring that white servants be purchased by slave owners) would fall most heavily on the aristocracy. In 1717, the ownership of one white man and ten Negroes in the County and Parish to be represented was urged as a qualification for election to the Commons House of Assembly. *Ibid.,* V, 294-95.

¹⁶ Act No. 383 in *Trott MS,* p. 701; also Cooper III, 14. *See* Appendix I.

¹⁷ *JCHA,* VI, 7. At this time it was provided also that those in Charles Town, "possessed of stock and cash amounting to one thousand Pounds should be obliged to keep a white person." The Council would have preferred the amount at £2,000. *CJ,* II, 23.

¹⁸ *JCHA,* VII, 151. As in the case of all bills where previous provisions were re-enacted, this one "for Importing and Imploying white Servants" sought to assure a more rigid conformity to the law. For debates, *see ibid.,* 152, 173, 269, 275-77, 284, and 310. This act was finally ratified on December 10, 1725.

¹⁹ Act No. 523, Cooper III, 272.

20 *JCHA*, VII, 432. Same confirmed in 1737. *Ibid.*, XI, 203-204.

21 *Ibid.*, XII, 126. Whichever basis was used, the white man for so many Negroes or for so many acres, he was employed, in at least a quasi-capacity, as an overseer of Negro slaves. On November 3, 1682, an Order in Council referring to the importation of whites into Barbados deprecated any restriction on the business as "a great misfortune to the trade of the Colonies, for they have no white men to superintend their negroes." *CSP, Colonial*, XI, 768i. The status of the servant-slave question in Barbados of the last quarter of the seventeenth century was that of Carolina in the second quarter of the eighteenth.

22 *CJ*, VII, 354.

23 Act No. 18, in Part II of *Trott MS*, p. 100. Section VIII of the same act provides for the attendance of the servant as soon as his time has expired. *See also*, Act No. 27, Cooper II, 12, and Act No. 508, Cooper III, 255. "The Practical Justice of the Peace" includes, under the caption "Militia", "the substance of such paragraphs of the present laws as contain the duties of those concerned in the execution of them." Section 17 reads: "Every servant of St. Philip and St. Michael (parishes), Charles Town, shall be allowed six months after being discharged from his servitude, to provide himself with the arms and furniture by this act directed an required, and during that time shall be exempted from the penalties inflicted by this act."

24 *LT*, Ia, 388.

25 *JCHA*, XIII, 472.

26 *Ibid.*, XVI, 112-13.

27 *Ibid.*, p. 150.

28 *Ibid.*, XX, 193. Two years later it was voted "that indented apprentices be exempted from doing Patrol service." *Ibid.*, XXI, 510.

29 Simpson, *op. cit.*, p. 195.

30 *JCHA*, VII, 285.

31 *Ibid.*, V, 90. *See also* the petition of Susanah Jordan, dated June 15, 1722, for a servant "killed in the public service." *CJ*, II, 24.

32 *JCHA*, V, 313.

33 *Ibid.*, p. 363.

34 *CJ*, VI, 15. On November 7, 1717, an order was drawn in favor of Col. Parris for "expences in sending men to take the runaway servants; they having been sent by the Governor's orders; and for the country's service." *JCHA*, V, 357. In the same volume of the House Journal are a number of interesting items of expense for clothing the public servants in garrison. *Ibid.*, pp. 175, 181, and 480. *Also see ibid.*, VI, 143, and *CJ*, II, 244.

35 *JCHA*, X, 454, and *XI*, 10-11.

36 *Ibid.*, XVIII, 263.

37 *Ibid.*, p. 329. In 1716 Nathaniel Snow petitioned for payment for "a white servant he had killed in the Public Service of the war." *Ibid.*, V, 178. In 1720 Jonathan Goodbee wanted three months' pay "for his servant-man John Peacock's service as a soldier." *Ibid.*, p. 444. In 1716, the House ordered that where such soldiers deserted, their masters be paid only what "was due at the time of such desertion." *Ibid.*, p. 175. At a later date, "every poor Freeman

or white Servant, who shall cheerfully and boldly oppose the common Enemy [at St. Augustine], and shall in Fight, happen to be maimed and dis-abled from Labour" shall, upon proper proof, be entitled to a yearly stipend "of *Twelve Pounds Proclamation* money." *Gazette,* April 4-11, 1740.

³⁸ *LT,* Ia, 684. Nevertheless, in times of external danger, proposals were made to use the Negroes as troops. In 1704 was passed "An Act for Raising and Enlisting Such Slaves as shall be thought Serviceable to this Province in time of Alarms." *See* Act No. 237, *Trott MS,* p. 242. Also similar acts were passed in 1707, *ibid.,* p. 313, and in 1712, *ibid.,* p. 606. In 1738, a bill providing for "the manner of Arming Slaves in case of Alarm and Invasion" was carried in the negative only in respect to their being armed "by the Public." *JCHA,* XI, 364. In 1741, proposals "for better protecting the Province" empowered "the Govr. or the Commander in chief for the time being to direct and order the Captains of the several Companys to inlist such number of male slaves (not to exceed one third of the number of white persons in their Companys) as the said Captains shall judge will be most serviceable in times of alarm and invasion." *JCHA,* XVI, 255. Just a year later, certificates were presented for such service performed by slaves. *Ibid.,* XVIII, 266-67. In 1747 an estimated savings of £1,127 on a total of £21,102 was possible because the service of Negroes was paid for at £12 currency per month, as against £15 for white men. *Ibid.,* XXII, 502.

³⁹ *LT,* II, 126. In January 1741 was presented the account of Hon. John Colleton "for sundry charges on the tryals of 67 Negroes who were concerned in the late intended insurrection in the Parish of St. John in the County of Colleton." *JCHA,* XIV, 139.

⁴⁰ *CJ,* V, 718.

⁴¹ *JCHA,* XVIII, 684-85.

⁴² *Ibid.,* XXV, 252.

⁴³ *PCR, 1753-1755,* p. 90.

⁴⁴ *Gazette,* March 2-9, 1738.

⁴⁵ *JCHA,* XXV, 251. Under the fourth head of this report, it was provided "that all Boats coming to Charlestown with a Loading equal to twenty Barrels of Rice shall not be suffered to do it without one white man attending her."

⁴⁶ *LT,* XXVII, 116 ff.

⁴⁷ *Vestry Books, Prince Frederick's, Winyaw,* I, 15-16.

⁴⁸ *JCHA,* XXXII, 211-12.

⁴⁹ Ruth Allison Hudnut and Hayes Baker Crothers, "Acadian Transients in South Carolina," *American Historical Review,* XLIII (1937-38), 500-513. (Quote p. 508.)

CHAPTER IV

¹ *CSP, Colonial,* XVI, 25.

² The two principal acts dealing with white servants were passed by the South Carolina legislature in 1717 and in 1744, just after the troubles with the Old Pretender and just before those with the Young Pretender.

³ *CSP, Colonial,* XII, 380-81, 402-04, 422, 441-42, 453, 2114-21, and 2124-25.

⁴ *Ibid.,* XII, 540. *See also ibid.,* 561, 561-i, iv, v, vi, 610.

[5] *Ibid.,* XIII, 228.

[6] *Gazette,* October 27, November 4 and 11, 1739.

[7] *Ibid.,* March 5, 12, 19, 1741.

[8] *LT,* XVIII, 191.

[9] *CSP, Colonial,* VII, 175.

[10] *Ibid.,* p. 881.

[11] Act No. 318, *Trott MS,* p. 501.

[12] *JCHA,* VII, 391. This was in December 1726.

[13] *PCR, 1727-1729,* p. 253.

[14] *JCHA,* XIV, 132.

[15] *CSP, Colonial,* XV, 1134.

[16] *Ibid.,* p. 1195.

[17] *Ibid.,* p. 1157.

[18] *Ibid.,* p. 1166. The people of St. Christophers were like-minded. In 1682 Christopher Jeaffreson petitioned on their behalf for the removal of the heavy security imposed on the importation of malefactors. *Ibid.,* XI, 800.

[19] *Ibid.,* XV, 1194.

[20] *Ibid.,* p. 1172.

[21] *Ibid.,* pp. 1189 and 1216.

[22] *Gazette,* Feb. 10, 1746.

[23] *CJ,* Oct. 27, 1955.

[24] *Ibid.*

[25] *Ibid.,* Jan. 6, 1956.

[26] *Ibid.,* Dec. 5, 1755.

[27] The three years after January 1, 1766.

[28] Nathaniel Russell to Rev. Ezra Stiles, Charles Town, July 19, 1767 in Gratz Collection, Pennsylvania Historical Society.

[29] *Laurens' Letters, 1767-1771,* p. 130.

[30] *Ibid.,* p. 152.

[31] *Ibid.,* pp. 166-69.

[32] *Ibid.,* p. 171.

[33] *Ibid.,* p. 182.

[34] Harriott Horry Ravenel, *Eliza Pinckney* (New York: Charles Scribner's Sons, 1928), pp. 124-25.

CHAPTER V

[1] Dates of *Gazette* appear on Table, page 4.

[2] Abbot Emerson Smith, *Colonists in Bondage* (Chapel Hill: University of North Carolina Press, 1947), pp. 21-22.

[3] Karl F. Geiser, "Redemptioners and Indentured Servants in the Colony and Commonwealth of Pennsylvania," Supplement to *Yale Review,* X (1901), 41.

[4] B. R. Carroll, *Historical Collections of South Carolina* (New York, 1836), II, 17. "When Adam Hover heard of the arival of the immigrants on one of the first ships, he came down from his home on Crims Creek with several of his friends 'to purchase some of them,' and meeting Barbara [Powmin] he forthwith engaged her for marriage." Robert L. Meriwether, *The Expansion*

of South Carolina, 1729-1765 (Kingsport: Southern Publishers, Inc., 1940), p. 152.

[5] *JCHA*, V, 381-87, 421.

[6] *Ibid.*, VII, 91, 231, 454-55.

[7] *Ibid.*, VII, 398.

[8] *Gazette*, July 19-26, 1735. As an alternative, these passengers might be carried on to Philadelphia, for an added Pistol per head. (Equal to £6.)

[9] *JCHA*, XXV, 87-89.

[10] Hans Jacob Riemensperger settled in South Carolina in 1736 with twenty-nine families. This is set forth in a petition to the King in Council, May 8, 1749. *LT*, XXIII, 299-302, 318. From the tale told, as above narrated, this sounds much like the reality of his story about the three thousand.

[11] *JCHA*, XXV, 12.

[12] David Ramsay, *History of South Carolina* (Trenton, 1785), I, 20.

[13] Chapman J. Milling (ed.), *Colonial South Carolina: Two Contemporary Descriptions by Governor James Glen and Doctor George Milligen-Johnston* (Columbia: University of South Carolina Press, 1951), pp. 136, 137.

[14] *Ibid.*, p. 138.

[15] *Gazette*, January 7, 14, 28, 1745.

[16] *Ibid.*, October 23, 30, 1751, and November 13, 1751.

[17] *Ibid.*, October 3, November 27, and December 4, 1752.

[18] *Ibid.*, January 29 to March 19, 1753.

[19] *Ibid.*, February 27, March 5, March 12, and March 26, 1744. This is but a special phase of the customary sale for debt. Compare the following Order of the House, dated August 28, 1702: "That any person absconding or deserting after he hath enlisted himself to be on the Said Expedition be fined in the Sum of Ten Pounds, and in Case he be not able to pay the Said fine to be sold a servant till the Said Sum of ten pounds be raised." *JCHA*, II, 19. In 1735 the following advertisement appeared in the *Gazette*: "Notice is hereby given, that a Young Man of about 24 or 25 Years of Age, now being Kept in Prison for a Debt of 180£, is willing to serve any Gentleman that will advance the said Sum for him, any reasonable time to his full Satisfaction and Contentment." *Gazette*, March 8, 1735.

[20] *Ibid.*, February 4 to 18, 1745, January 15 to 22, 1750, February 5 to 19, 1750, February 13 to 27, 1742, September 1 to 27, 1752, December 4, 1751 to January 22, 1752, November 30 to December 14, 1734, October 17, 21, November 7, December 5, 12, 1754, and October 8 to 15, 1772. Numerous cards appeared announcing sales to take place on shipboard. *See ibid.*, September 30, 1732, June 9, 23, 1733, May 15 to 29, 1736, January 20 to February 1, 1746, November 27 to December 4, 1749, and December 3 to 17, 1750.

[21] *Laurens' Letters, 1755-1757*, p. 116.

[22] *CJ*, V, 235.

[23] *Ibid.*, VI, 31.

[24] *Ibid.*, pp. 32-33.

[25] *Ibid.*, VI, 33. In this particular case, an agreement was reached by a joint committee of both houses, favorable to the petitioners. *Ibid.*, VI, 33-35.

The following memorandum is attached: "The names of the Swiss, who have not paid their passage &c:

John Mathias and wife 2	Eighteen passages, under In-
Ulrich Speri Smith 1	dentures, at £6. p. Head. .£108. 0.0
Jacob Viterling 1	One do., per note 3.10.0
Jacob Galman and nine children . .10	
Jacob Spuhl 1	£111.10.0
Herman Christian Dittering & wife. 2	Exchange 600 Pct. 669. 0.0
Henry Segrist 1	Carolina Currency ....£780.10.0"
Henry Ealder, Per Note 1	

19

[26] *Ibid.*, VII, 61-63. *See also JCHA*, XI, 216, 244-45. So frequent did such cases become that distinct provision was made for the legal indenture of this particular class. *See* Sec. 1, Act of 1744.

[27] *CJ*, V, 56.

[28] *Ibid.*, V, 682. In May 1735 Samuel Eveleigh, "Merchant in Carolina," wrote to the Provost Marshal of the Province that the Irish Protestants settled at Williamsburgh eighteen months before, "planted and made very good crops so far that they had corn enough for themselves and 500 Bushels to spare." He commented favorably also upon the "Switzers", saying a correspondent of his advises "they were industrious and settling apace." *LT*, XVII, 339-40.

[29] *Ibid.*, II, 37.

[30] *JCHA*, XXIII, 421. In November 1726, of a total "imposition" of £8,900 for the establishment of five new forts, £5,000 was levied on Negroes imported, at £5 per head. *JCHA*, VII, 375.

[31] H. A. M. Smith, "Purrysburgh", *The South Carolina Historical and Genealogical Magazine*, X (1909), 18. *Also see JCHA*, VII, 488-90, 509. Verner Crane has written: "The most striking illustration of the proprietary blight was the collapse of the first attempt of the Swiss *entrepreneur*, Jean Pierre Purry, to settle a Swiss colony upon the southern margins of South Carolina." Verner W. Crane, *The Southern Frontier, 1670-1732* (Ann Arbor: The University of Michigan Press, 1955), p. 283.

[32] H. A. M. Smith, *op. cit.*, p. 192.

[33] This essay is printed in Force's *Tracts*, II (1838). A report of the Committee on Rebuilding Charles Town, made to the House on December 15, 1740, gives the day's wage of a master-carpenter as £2.0.0, of a journeyman as £1.5.0, of apprentices during the first year £0.7.6, during the second year £0.10.0, during the third year £0.15.0, and during the fourth year £1.0.0. *JCHA*, XIV, 44. Exchange in 1734 was charged at 600% (as between sterling and Carolina money), but even then the wages paid in the colony were a great inducement to immigrate.

[34] B. R. Carroll, *Historical Collections of South Carolina* (New York, 1836), II, 122-23.

[35] *Gazette*, September 23, 1732.

[36] H. A. M. Smith, *op. cit.*, p. 193.

[37] *CJ*, V, 385, 505.

[38] *Gazette*, April 26, 1735.

[39] *Ibid.*, July 12-19, 1735.

[40] *LT*, XVII, 227-28. In March 1743 further items, aggregating £3,313. 12s. 6d., appeared against the Purrysburg account, and are deducted from township funds. *JCHA*, XVIII, 589.

[41] *CJ*, V, 214, 222.

[42] *LT*, XVII, 228. Thomas Lowndes had advised, several years previously, in a letter dated August 7, 1729, that the Pennsylvania Assembly had lately laid a duty of forty shillings per head upon every Palatine arriving in the Province. *Ibid.*, XIII, 377. Virginia also levied import duties on servants. *CSP, Colonial*, XIX, 1040.

[43] Gilbert P. Voigt, "The German and German-Swiss Element in South Carolina, 1732-1752," *Bulletin of the University of South Carolina*, Number 113 (September 1922), p. 8.

[44] General Assembly, Charlestown, July 25, 1761, Records of the States of the U.S.A., 1761-1775, A microfilm compilation prepared by the Library of Congress in association with the U.N.C., collected and edited under direction of William Sumner Jenkins, 1949.

[45] *Ibid.*

[46] *CJ*, September 27, 1752.

[47] *Ibid.*, January 20, 1752.

[48] *Ibid.*, March 17, 1752.

[49] *Ibid.*, April 24, 1752.

[50] *Ibid.*, November 22, 1752.

[51] *Ibid.*, November 24, 1752.

[52] *Ibid.*, November 25, 1752.

[53] *Ibid.*, November 28, 1952.

[54] *Ibid.*, January 31, 1753.

[55] *Ibid.*, March 8, 1753.

[56] *Ibid.*

[57] *Ibid.*

[58] *Ibid.*, February 21, 1753, and May 14, 1754.

[59] General Duty Act, June 14, 1751, and an Act passed October 7, 1752, for altering and amending the sixth and seventh paragraphs of the Act commonly called the General Duty Act.

[60] Janie Revill, *A Compilation of the Original Lists of Protestant Immigrants to South Carolina, 1763-1773* (Columbia, 1939).

[61] *Ibid.*, January 14, 1745/46, pp. 13-14.

[62] *Ibid.*, January 10, 1745/46, p. 6.

[63] *Ibid.*, January 19, 1745/46, pp. 3-4.

[64] *Ibid.*, July 6, 1752.

[65] *Ibid.*, June 1, 1752.

[66] *Ibid.*, January 27, 1752.

[67] *Ibid.*, June 16, 1752.

[68] Wallace, *op. cit.*, pp. 153-54.

[69] *City Gazette,* August 30, 1805.
[70] *CJ,* August 31, 1752.
[71] *Ibid.,* October 3, 1752.
[72] *Ibid.,* September 8, 1755.
[73] Laurence Scott Barringer, *Family Facts for the Future* (Columbia: The R. L. Bryan Company, 1958), p. 98.
[74] *CJ,* January 5, 1756.
[75] *Ibid.,* January 5, 1756.
[76] *Ibid.,* September 1, 1755.
[77] *Ibid.,* January 6, 1755.
[78] *Ibid.,* December 2, 1755.
[79] *Ibid.,* December 2, 1755.
[80] *Ibid.,* December 1, 1755.
[81] *Ibid.,* November 17, 1755.
[82] *Ibid.,* January 2, 1754.
[83] *Ibid.,* October 22, 1754.
[84] *Ibid.,* November 5, 1754.
[85] *Ibid.,* January 7, 1755.
[86] *Ibid.,* January 7, 1755.
[87] *Ibid.,* May 14, 1755.
[88] *Ibid.,* December 2, 1755.
[89] *Ibid.,* November 3, 1755.
[90] *Ibid.,* December 2, 1755.
[91] *Ibid.,* August 6, 1754.

CHAPTER VI

[1] *PCR (1767-1771),* pp. 332-33.
[2] *Records of the Secretary of the Province,* p. 24.
[3] *PCR (1727-1729),* p. 238.
[4] *Ibid., (1694-1704),* p. 291.
[5] *Ibid.,* p. 292.
[6] *Ibid.,* p. 292. For other indentures, *see Records of the Secretary of the Province,* February 23, p. 167. *Also PCR (1694-1704),* pp. 378-79; *Ibid. (1729-1731),* p. 229; *Ibid. (1746-1749),* pp. 214-15; *Ibid. (1751-1754),* p. 548; *Ibid. (1754-1758),* p. 74; *Ibid. (1774-1779),* p. 499. Of interest among Negro indentures is that of Jack Cutler, who entered indenture in London and was brought to South Carolina. *PCR (1729-1731),* p. 41.
[7] *Records of the Register of the Province,* September 20, 1682.
[8] *Cooper,* II, 30-31.
[9] *Ibid.,* III, 15. See Section 1 of Act in Appendix I.
[10] *PCR (1722-1726),* pp. 272-73.

CHAPTER VII

[1] *Journal of Grand Council (1671-1680),* pp. 22-23.
[2] *Ibid.,* p. 50.

[3] Act No. 34, *Cooper*, II, 23.

[4] Act No. 60, *Ibid.*, 53.

[5] Act No. 383, *Ibid.*, III, 16.

[6] Act No. 710, *Ibid.*, p. 623.

[7] "[The following fees, however,] the several Justices of the Peace, officers and other persons are empowered to take:

	Proclamation money		
	£	s.	d.
To the justice before whom an indenture is executed	0	1	0
To the justice for his certificate of service, upon refusal to execute an indenture	0	2	6
To the Governour for the certificate of the age of each servant	0	5	0
To the justices if certified by them	0	2	6
To the justices for an order of conviction of each servant's laying violent hands on his master, mistress or overseer, each	0	2	6
To the Governour for his decree, on an appeal from the justices	0	5	0
To the person for apprehending each servant	1	0	0
To mileage to the justices house, per mile	0	0	3
To the justices for examination and order thereon	0	2	0
To the constable, per mile, from where he receives, to the place of delivery of each servant, besides ferriage and diet.	0	0	3
To the Marshal or Warden of the Workhouse, for receiving and discharging each servant	0	2	6
To the Marshal or Warden for whipping each servant	0	2	0
To diet, per day, for each servant, allowing at least 1-lb. of bread and 1-lb. of meat, wholesale provisions	0	1	3

Simpson, *op. cit.*, p. 234. The committee report recommending these fees contained the additional item of 4s., payable to the constable, for whipping each servant. *JCHA*, XVIII, 381-82.

[8] Act No. 383, *Cooper*, III, 16.

[9] A number of factors must be considered in the evaluation of a servant's time, such as age, trade, date of indenture &c. The best evidence is the appraisal of such in the records of the Probate Court; but, unfortunately, they are comparatively few, very general in character, and show considerable divergence:

	£.	s.	d.
1733, Colleton County, 3 yrs. for a man, annual average	6.13.	4.	
1733, Charleston, same for a woman annual average	16.13.	4.	
1742, A shoemaker, 3 and ¾ yrs. time annual average	16. 0.	0.	
1754, Georgetown, planter's man annual average	24. 0.	0.	
1754, Three years of boy's time annual average	13. 6.	8.	
1755, A Dutch boy, 6 years time annual average	8. 6.	8.	
1757, A Dutch cooper, 2 and 2/3 yrs. time annual average	18.15.	0.	

PCR (1732-1736), pp. 19 and 42; *ibid. (1741-1743)*, p. 168; *ibid. (1753-1756)*, pp. 224, 249, and 298; *ibid. (1756-1758)*, p. 64.

[10] Act No. 383, *Cooper*, III, 17.

[11] *Ibid.*

[12] Act No. 710, *ibid.*, p. 624.

[13] Act No. 383, *ibid.*, p. 18.

[14] Act No. 710, *ibid.*, p. 625.

[15] Act No. 383, *ibid.*, p. 17.

[16] Simpson, *op. cit.*, p. 103.

[17] *Cooper*, III, 18.

[18] This must have been quite a responsibility for the marshal. One jail delivery in 1741 resulted in the escape of five servants.

[19] Act No. 710, *Cooper*, III, 625.

[20] *Ibid.*

[21] *Journal of Grand Council (1671-1680)*, p. 14.

[22] *Ibid.*, pp. 33-34.

[23] Act No. 126, *Cooper*, II, 105.

[24] "[Following is a copy of the Calendar of] a Court of General Sessions, Assize and general Goal Delivery, held at Charles City and port on Wednesday, the 17th day of October, Anno Dom. 1722:

	Crimes	Pleas	Verdicts	Judgements Current Proc. Money	Money
Matthew Quash	Assault	Not Guilty	Guilty....£	2.10s.	£ 10.
Adam Stuart	Assault	Not Guilty	Guilty....£	2.10s.	£ 10.
John Ellis	Assault	Not Guilty	Guilty....£	2.10s.	£ 10.
Edmund Porter	Assault	Not Guilty	Guilty....£	0.10s.	£ 2.
Matthew Quash, on 2d indictment	Assault	Not Guilty	Guilty....£	2.10s.	£ 10.
Richard Perry	Felony	Not Guilty	Not Guilty	......	....
Richard Perry	Misdemeanor,	committed, submitted, and in court, on trial — craved clemency		£ 6. 5s.	£ 25.
Robert Quash	Assault	Guilty		£ 1. 5s.	£ 5.
William Rhett	Scandalous words vs his Excellency, the Gov.	Not Guilty	Guilty....£100.		£500.
Hill Croft	Misdemeanor	Not Guilty	Guilty....£ 12.10s.		£ 50.
Timothy Bellamy	Assault	Not Guilty	Guilty....£	2.10s.	£ 10.
Henry Nelson	Nuisance	Guilty		£ 2.10s.	£ 10.
Thomas Witten	Unlicensed Tavern	Guilty		£ 0. 5s.	£ 1.

LT, X. 14.

[25] Act No. 383, *Cooper*, III, 19.

[26] Act No. 710, *ibid.*, p. 628.

[27] Act No. 383, *ibid.*, p. 20.

[28] *Ibid.*

[29] *JCHA*, V, 234.

³⁰ *JCHA*, V, 300. Leniency was not uncommon. On June 15, 1724, the Governor signed "a free pardon" for Alexander Robertson, who with his wife had been convicted as "accessorys in felony," on condition that Robertson would serve in one of his Majesty's Garrisons. When this had been agreed to, it was found that the man could not so serve, because of lame hands. So application was made, and a full pardon was granted. *CJ*, II, 265 and 292. In February 1740 the House petitioned the Governor to order the Provost Marshal to put one Randall who was suffering with a sore foot "in a more convenient room than that where he at present is; as also to supply him with convenient necessarys And this House will take care to make provision for payment of what Expence shall attend the same." *JCHA*, XII, 304-05.

³¹ *JCHA*, V, 301.

³² *PCR (1754-1758)*, p. 48.

³³ Act No. 314, *Trott*, p. 462.

³⁴ Note grant of £80 each to the owners of four Negroes who had been executed by public order. *JCHA*, II, 156-157.

³⁵ *Gazette*, June 17, 1745.

³⁶ *Ibid.*, March 31-April 7, 1759.

³⁷ *JCHA*, XII, 18. For real cruelty in the punishment of slaves *see* Antigua: planning to run away—leg cut off; Antigua: mutinous behaviour—burned to ashes; Barbados: threatening Xians—burned alive; Montserrat: Theft of nine pigs—cut to pieces, bowels burned, quarter hung in public view; Montserrat: absent for three months—"broken in pieces"; Montserrat: theft of 12d—hanged and quarters set up. *CSP, Colonial*, XII, 1189 and 1193; XI, 1475; XIV, 520; XVII, 437 and 524.

³⁸ A reward was offered for the return of "A Free Negro Fellow, named *Johny Holmes*, bred a Wheelright and Carpenter, well known at *Goose Creek*, *Wassamssaw* and *Charlestown*, being lately an indented Servant with Nicholas Trott. . . ." *Gazette*, November 6-13, 20, and 27, 1736. In 1717, Thomas Cutler freed "Jne Gambo a negro man commonly called Jack Cutler—he is a free negroe haveing faithfully Served out his Time with me four Years According to the Contract Agreed upon in London." *PCR (1729-1731)*, p. 41. In at least one instance, a free Negro appears as the owner of a slave. *PCR (1754-1758)*, p. 406.

³⁹ In 1672, Robert Lewis was ordered to pay Col. West two bushels of Indian corn, because he had received one bushel from the latter's servant. *Journal Grand Council (1671-1680)*, p. 52. See *JCHA*, XX, 112.

⁴⁰ *JCHA*, XX, 112.

⁴¹ *See* Appendixes I and II.

⁴² *Ibid.* (*See* Appendix I.)

⁴³ *Gazette*, March 23-30 and April 6 and 13, 1734.

⁴⁴ *Ibid.*, March 2-9, 1734.

⁴⁵ Act No. 383, *Cooper*, III, 16.

⁴⁶ Act No. 60, *ibid.*, II, 53.

⁴⁷ *Journal of Grand Council (1692)*, pp. 34-35.

⁴⁸ *Ibid. (1671-1680)*, p. 52.

⁴⁹ *Ibid.*, p. 62.
⁵⁰ *Ibid. (1692)*, p. 36.
⁵¹ Simpson, *op. cit.*, p. 231.

CHAPTER VIII

¹ The age was, of course, harsh. A letter of 1665 recites the case of "four young men scourged by the hangman through Edinburgh, burnt behind the ear, and delivered up to be sent to Barbados, for abusing James Scott, a minister at Ancram, in time of sermon." *CSP, Colonial,* V, 1113.

² *Ibid.*, X, 1334.

³ *Journal of Grand Council (1671-1680)*, pp. 52 and 62, and *ibid. (1692)*, pp. 34-36.

⁴ *JCHA*, XII, 288.

⁵ *Laurens' Letters (1767-1771)*, p. 298.

⁶ *CSP, Colonial,* XIX, 1103.

⁷ *PCR (1732-1737)*, p. 415.

⁸ *Ibid. (1752-1756)*, p. 466.

⁹ *Ibid. (1761-1777)*, p. 209.

¹⁰ *Ibid.*, p. 542.

¹¹ *Ibid. (1740-1747)*, p. 385.

¹² *Gazette,* February 19, 26 and March 4, 1732.

¹³ *Ibid.*, February 23, 1734.

¹⁴ *Ibid.*, September 7-14, 14-21, and 28-October 5, 1734.

¹⁵ *Ibid.*, August 30 and September 6 and 13, 1735.

¹⁶ *Ibid.*, May 22 and 29 and June 5, 1736.

¹⁷ *Supplement to Gazette,* February 3, 1757.

¹⁸ *Gazette,* September 27 and October 4 and 11, 1742.

¹⁹ The *Gazette* of December 10 and 24, 1753 advertised: "Three years Time of a *Dutch* servant, a bricklayer, and his wife who understands a dairy and raising poultry, with three sons, one of which has 12 years, another 10 years, and the other 8 years to serve."

²⁰ *Gazette,* November 21 and 28, 1743.

²¹ *Ibid.*, January 8 and 15, 1754.

²² *Ibid.*, August 15 and 27, 1753. Among the papers recorded in the Probate Court is a letter from a Quaker (dated Barbados, 1679), who mentions his ownership of four Negroes and a white servant. *PCR (1672-1692)*, p. 39.

²³ *Gazette,* August 4, 11, and 18, 1733.

²⁴ *Ibid.*, August 9 and 23, 1733.

²⁵ This same price was offered for the return of a Negro, dead or alive, to which ferocious announcement was appended a note to the effect that if the fugitive returned he would be forgiven. *See ibid.*, March 23, 1752.

²⁶ *Ibid.*, May 16 and 25 and June 1, 1748.

²⁷ *Ibid.*, July 20-27, 1734.

²⁸ Butler: "British Convicts Shipped to American Colonies." The above anecdote was quoted from *London Magazine,* XLII, 311. The Butler article appears on page 29, in volume II, *AHR*.

CHAPTER IX

[1] *Gazette,* June 18 to July 2, 1753. Abraham had evidently not always been a model servant, for Mr. Sommers once published a notice warning all persons from entertaining him or selling him liquor. *Ibid.,* April 6, 1752.

[2] *Ibid.,* June 11, 1754.

[3] *Ibid.,* February 1, 1759.

[4] *Ibid.,* February 1, 1768.

[5] *Ibid.,* September 17, 1772.

[6] *Ibid.,* May 3, 1754.

[7] *Ibid.,* November 12, 1772.

[8] *Ibid.,* Supplement December 3, 1772.

[9] Richard Walsh, *Charleston's Sons of Liberty* (Columbia: University of South Carolina Press, 1959), p. 18.

[10] Frederick Law Olmsted, *A Journey in the Seaboard Slave States* (New York: Dix and Edwards, 1856), pp. 465-66.

[11] Henry A. M. Smith, *The Baronies of South Carolina* (Charleston: The South Carolina Historical Society, 1931), pp. 7, 19, 29, 37, 50, 57, 91, and 112.

[12] Robert L. Meriwether, *The Expansion of South Carolina, 1729-1765* (Kingsport: Southern Publishers, Inc., 1940).

[13] *Ibid.,* p. 181.

[14] Albert B. Faust, *The German Element in the United States* (Boston: Houghton Mifflin Company, 1909).

[15] Charles A. Hanna, *The Scotch-Irish* (New York: A. P. Putnam's Sons, 1902).

[16] Henry Jones Ford, *The Scotch-Irish in America* (Princeton: Princeton University Press, 1915).

[17] *A State of the Province of Georgia* (London, 1740), p. 18.

[18] Richard J. Hooker (ed.), *The Carolina Backcountry on the Eve of the Revolution* (Chapel Hill: University of North Carolina Press, 1953), pp. 239-40.

[19] William A. Schaper, "Sectionalism and Representation in South Carolina," *Annual Report of the American Historical Association for the Year 1900* (Washington, 1901), pp. 245-46.

[20] *Ibid.,* p. 248.

[21] *Ibid.,* p. 251.

[22] *Ibid.,* p. 379.

[23] *Ibid.,* p. 249.

[24] Ulrich B. Phillips, "The South Carolina Federalists," *The American Historical Review,* XIV, 529-30.

APPENDIX I

An Act for the Better Governing and Regulating White Servants

(This is Act No. 383 of 1717.—See TROTT MS: pp. 701 to 715; and COOPER (Columbia, S. C.: A. D. Johnson, 1838), III, 14 to 20.

* * *

"Whereas, there has of late arrived in this Province great numbers of white servants, which for want of sufficient rules to order, direct and govern them, have proved of bad consequence to their masters, owners and overseers; for remedy of which for the future,

"I. *Be it enacted* by his Excellency John Lord Carteret, Palatine, and the rest of the true and absolute Lords and Proprietors of the Province of Carolina, by and with the advice and consent of the rest of the members of the General Assembly, now met at Charlestown for the South and West part of this Province, and by the authority of the same, That all servants shall serve according to his contract or indentures; and where there is no contract or indentures, servants under the age of sixteen years at their arrival in this Province, shall serve until they are of the age of one and twenty years; and if they be above the age of sixteen years, they shall serve five years; and at the expiration of the time aforesaid, shall receive from their master, mistress or employer, a certificate of their freedom on demand; and whoever shall refuse without good cause to give such certificate to any servant whose time is expired, shall forfeit forty shillings for every refusal, to be recovered by the party injured, as is directed in the Act for the Trial of small and mean causes; Provided, that nothing in this Act be construed to extend to any person whatsoever that is brought into this Province, that has not obliged themselves by some contracts to become servants, but such person or persons so brought in, shall pay or cause to be paid to the importer, for his passage, in twenty days after his arrival, in the current money of this Province, allowing for the difference of the exchange of money of the place from whence they were exported, according to the usual rate of passages from such port or place to this Province.

"II. *And be it further enacted* by the authority aforesaid, That all servants brought or transported out of any of his Majestty's col-

[109]

onies in America into this Province, shall compleat their servitude here, which they ought to have served in the said colonies, and no more.

"III. *And be it further enacted* by the authority aforesaid, That every master, mistress or other person whatsoever, owning or keeping any servants, whether by virtue of transportation, purchase or otherwise, shall within six months after the receiving such servant into their custody within this Province (except he, she or they claim but five years service of such servants) bring the said servants before the Governor of this Province, or any one of the Lords Proprietors deputies, or any two Justices of the Peace, who are hereby authorized to judge or determine of the age of such servants brought before them, and to return a certificate of such their determination, into the Secretary's office of this Province; and every owner as aforesaid, neglecting or refusing to bring such servant or servants as is before directed, shall not claim above five years service of such servant or servants, any thing herein contained to the contrary notwithstanding.

"IV. And to prevent disputes that may arise about what time servants time of servitude, whether by indenture or otherwise, shall commence, *Be it enacted* by the authority aforesaid, that all servants transported into this Province, whether by indenture or otherwise, or so bound or adjudged as aforesaid, shall commence their time of servitude from the first anchoring of the vessel within this Province in which they were imported.

"V. *And be it further enacted* by the authority aforesaid, That it shall not be lawful for the master or owner of any servants to make any bargain or agreement with his servant to serve him any longer time, before the time of his first service by indenture or otherwise is expired and fully ended; and every such bargain or indenture made by any servant during the time of his service, shall be void and not any ways obligatory on such servant for longer time than by his first indenture, or according to this Act.

"VI. And whereas divers ill-disposed persons do secretely and covertly truck and trade with other men's servants and apprentices, who to the great injury of their masters are thereby induced and encouraged to steal, purloyn and embezzel their master's goods; *Be it therefore enacted,* That what person or persons soever shall buy, sell, trade or barter with any servant for any commodity whatsoever, without lycence or consent of such servant's master or mistress, he or they so offending against the premisses, shall forfeit to the master or mistress of such servants, treble the value of the things traded for, bought or sold, and also ten pounds current money to him or them that shall inform for the same, to be within twenty-five days after the fact committed, recovered by such master, mistress or informer as will sue for the same, by action of debt in any court of record within this Province; and in case the person or persons so offending shall not be able to satisfy the same, then such person or persons shall give bond with security, for his or their good behaviour, and to appear at the next general sessions of the peace and general gaol delivery, where, upon conviction by confession or sufficient witnesses, the offender shall be punished by whipping on the bare back, at the watchouse in Charlestown, and all such contracts made with such servants are hereby declared to be utterly null and void.

"VII. *And be it further enacted* by the authority aforesaid, That if any servant or hired labourer shall lay violent hands, or beat or strike his or her master, mistress or overseer, and be convicted thereof by confession or evidence of his fellow servant or otherwise, before any two Justices of the Peace in this Province, the said Justices of the Peace are hereby required and authorized to order such servant or labourer to serve his or her master or mistress, or their assigns, any time not exceeding six months, without any wages, after his or her time by indenture or otherwise is expired; or such corporal punishment, to be inflicted by the hands of the constable or some other white person, not exceeding twenty-one stripes, as they shall in their discretion think fitting, according to the nature of the crime.

"VIII. *And be it further enacted* by the authority aforesaid, That any servant or servants unlawfully absenting him, her or themselves, from his, her or their said master, mistress or overseer, shall for every such day's absence, serve one week, and so in proportion for a longer or shorter time, the whole punishment not to exceed two years over and above the time he or she was to serve by indenture or as is otherwise directed by this Act, and shall satisfy or pay to his, her or their master or mistress, all such cost and charges as shall be laid out and expended for their taking up, by servitude; and the master or mistress of any runaway servant, that intend to take the benefit of this Act, shall as soon as he or she hath recovered him, her or them, carry the said persons before the next Justice of the Peace, and there declare upon oath, or prove by one or more sufficient witnesses, the time of his, her, or their absence, and the charge he or she hath been at in his, her or their recovery, which Justice of the Peace thereupon shall grant his certificate, and the Governour and Council, on that certificate, shall pass judgment for the time he shall serve for his absence.

"IX. And whereas divers persons that by identure, contract for wages or otherwise, being servants, do many times run away to remote plantations, and there being unknown are entertained by others for wages or shares; for prevention whereof for the future, and for the better discovery of runaways, *Be it enacted* by the authority aforesaid, That all servants at the expiration of their time, shall carry the certificate obtained as is before in this Act directed, to the next Justice of the Peace to his last place of dwelling, and get the said certificate indorsed and attested by the said Justice of the Peace, who is hereby required to endorse the same without fee or reward, which certificate so attested shall be sufficient warrant for any person to entertain him, her or them in their service; and whoever shall entertain or harbour any servant running away from his master's service, and not having a certificate as aforesaid, shall pay to the master of such servant for every day and night two pounds current money, for all the time he shall harbour or entertain him, so that the whole exceed not treble the value of the servant's time remaining to be served with the master or mistress. Provided, that if such runaway servant shall forge a certificate, and by that means procure himself entertainment, the person entertaining him shall be free from the fine, but the servant or any other person for him forging the certificate, shall be punished for his forgery upon conviction, by standing in the pillory in Charlestown, as the Chief Justice shall direct.

"X. *And be it further enacted* by the authority aforesaid, That if the master or owner of any servant shall at the expiration of the time of any such servant to them belonging, denying or refuse, without just cause for the same, to give a certificate to the same servant as is in this Act directed, such master or owner, for every such denial or refusal, shall forfeit the sum of two pounds current money, to be recovered as in the Act for Trial of Small and Mean Causes is directed, for the use of the poor of the parish where such offence is committed.

"XI. *And be it further enacted* by the authority aforesaid, That if any freeman shall by any contract agree with any person or persons, and before the time agreed for be accomplished shall depart to another, he shall perform the tenor of his contract first made and pay the apparent damages that shall arise from his breach of covenant, and shall after that is satisfied be liable to the payment of what damages any other contractor with him shall recover of him by law; and whosoever shall employ any free person (handicraft tradesmen excepted) without a certificate from the last employer, of the performance of his or their last bargain or contract, shall forfeit twenty-five pounds, to be recovered by action of debt, in any court of record in this Province, by the person suffering thereby.

"XII. *And be it further enacted* by the authority aforesaid, That in case any servant shall run away in company of any slaves, that every such servant so running away in company with any slave or slaves, shall upon conviction thereof at the general sessions of the peace and gaol delivery of this Province, be deemed a felon, and the punishment of a felon be inflicted on him accordingly, without benefit of clergy.

"XIII. And to prevent the barbarous usage of servants by cruel masters, *Be it enacted* by the authority aforesaid, That every master or mistress shall provide for his servants competent diet, clothing and lodging, and that he shall not exceed the bounds of moderation in correcting them beyond the merit of their offences; and that it shall be lawful for any servant, upon any master or mistress whatsoever, or overseer by order or consent of any such master or mistress, denying and not providing sufficient meat, drink, lodging and clothing, or shall unreasonably burthen them beyond their strength with labour, or debar them of their necessary rest and sleep, or excessively beat or abuse them, to repair to the next Justice of Peace to make his or her complaint; and if the said Justice of Peace shall find by just proof that the said servant's complaint is just, he is hereby impowered for the first offence to admonish the said master, mistress or overseer; and for the second offence, upon complaint made to any two Justices, and upon due proof, the said two Justices may levy and distrain, by a warrant under their hand and seal directed to the next constable, any sum not exceeding ten pounds, to be disposed of for the use of the poor of the parish where the offence is committed; and for the third offence, any two Justices of the Peace shall then be and they are hereby authorized and impowered to associate together, and to sell and dispose of the time of such servant to any other white person for such money as they can get for the same, which shall be paid to the churchwardens of that parish, for the use of the poor; saving the right of the master or mistress of appealing to the Governour and Council from the sentence or judgment of two such Justices of the Peace for the disposal or turning over such servant.

"XIV. *And be it further enacted by the authority aforesaid,* That if any punch-house keeper, vintner or other person whatsoever, shall entertain any man's servant any time, if the said servant shall be drunk, trade or game during such time, he or they so offending shall forfeit forty shillings, to be recovered as in the Act for small and mean causes is directed.

"XV. And for the encouragement of all persons, to seize or take up runaway servants, *it is further enacted* by the authority aforesaid, that all and every person as aforesaid, seizing or taking up such runaway servants, shall (if their master or mistress be known) convey the said runaway servants to their master or mistress at their usual place of residence, and for their service receive the sum of twenty shillings for every runaway servant so taken up, and six pence for every mile; but if the said master or mistress be not known, or live very remote, then the said runaway servant is to be conveyed to the common gaol in Charlestown, which said gaoler is hereby impowered and commanded to receive such runaway and runaways, and to pay the bringer the sum aforesaid, for every such runaway servant brought to him, on penalty of forty shillings; and that it shall and may be lawful for the marshal to detain and keep in custody the bodies of all such runaway servants so brought to him, until the master or mistress of them, or their assigns, shall pay unto him the full sum which he hath so paid for them, together with the diet as long as they shall continue in the marshal's custody, also two shillings and six pence for every twenty-four hours the said runaway servant hath been in custody; and the said marshal shall within ten days after the receiving such servant or servants, send a message to their master or mistress, at the charge of such master or mistress, and if the marshal shall neglect to send as is above directed, he is hereby made liable to the same fines and penalties as persons are that entertain white servants; and if the said marshal shall suffer any runaway servant so brought to him, to escape before he or she be duly delivered to his master or mistress, or his or their assigns, that then the said marshal shall pay unto the said master or mistress of the said runaway servant so much as he shall be condemned in by verdict of a jury at common law; and it is also lawful for any person to take up any suspected persons and carry him or her to any Justice of Peace to be examined.

"XVI. *And be it further enacted* by the authority aforesaid, That if a master of any runaway servants, or any Justice of the Peace, order any corporal punishment to be inflicted on runaway servants, it shall not deprive the master of the satisfaction allowed by this law, the one being as necessary to reclaim them from further persisting in that idle course, as the other is just to repair the damages sustained by their masters. And if any servant shall offend more than twice in running away, it is hereby ordered that every constable into whose hands the said runaway shall by any Justice of the Peace's warrant be first committed, shall cause him to be severely whipped, and convey him to the next constable towards his master's house, who is to give him the like correction, and so every constable through whose precincts he passeth to do the like.

"XVII. And whereas by several laws of this Province, the breaches against the same are punishable by fines, and as servants during their service are wholly uncapable of paying, and might be encouraged to attempt it should their punishment be respited until their time of service is expired; *Be it therefore enacted* by the authority aforesaid, That in all cases where a freeman is punishable by fines, a servant shall receive corporal punishment, for every twenty shillings fine, nine lashes, and so many such several punishments as there is twenty shillings included in the fine, unless the master or other acquaintance shall redeem them by making payment. And if any person shall by procurement of the servant, upon promise and agreement for future service, pay the fine, and release him from punishment, such agreement made shall bind such servant to performance, after his time by indenture be expired, any thing herein contained to the contrary notwithstanding.

"XVIII. And whereas it sometimes happens, that servants imported into this Province, being ignorant of the customs here, do sometimes bring in with them a small parcel of goods, or have them afterwards by their friends; *Be it therefore enacted* by the authority aforesaid, That all servants bringing in goods with them, not being their own wearing apparel, or having them consigned to them during the time of their service, shall have a property in their own goods, and dispose of the same for their own future advantage.

"XIX. *And be it further enacted* by the authority aforesaid, That if any person inhabiting and residing in this Province, shall turn away any sick or infirm servant, under pretence of freedom or otherwise, and such servant shall die for want of relief, or become chargeable to any parish, the offender shall forfeit the sum of twenty pounds current money, to the use of the parish where such death or charges shall happen, to be recovered by the church-wardens, by action of debt, in any court of record in this Province, and also receive the said servant if living, and him to maintain during the whole time the said servant had to serve; but if any servant through wilful misbehaviour, shall happen to have the pox, yaws, broken bones, impediment or imprisonment, he or she shall serve their master or mistress double the time thereby neglected, and also all charges occasioned by reason thereof, after their time by indenture or otherwise be expired; and also all masters or mistresses of servants who shall receive unjust molestation by complaints or suits of law, shall have the same remedy for their expences and loss of time.

"XX. *And be it further enacted* by the authority aforesaid, That if any free-man of this Province shall at any time hereafter beget a woman-servant with child, he shall (upon due proof thereof according to the directions of the Act relating to Bastardy) give good security to save the parish harmless, and as a further punishment for his offence, and for and towards satisfaction of the master or mistress of such servant, shall forfeit and pay unto the said master or mistress the sum of ten pounds current money, and shall likewise provide for the maintenance of the said servant during her lying-in, and for the child during the time of the servitude of the said servant, and in case of failure therein shall serve the master or mistress of such servant also during the time she had to serve from the time of her delivery, or shall procure one in his or their stead, that shall be obliged so to do. And in case one servant shall beget another with child, then the man-servant shall after the expiration of his term, serve the master or mistress of the woman-servant, during the time she had to serve from the time of her delivery; and if any man shall marry without his master or mistress's consent, he shall serve one year for such offence, or forfeit the sum of twenty pounds; but if any free-man shall marry a servant, he shall be liable to pay the full value of the said servant to her master or mistress, and she shall be free.

"XXI. *And be it further enacted* by the authority aforesaid, That any white woman, whether free or a servant, that shall suffer herself to be got with child by a negro or other slave or free negro, such woman so begot with child as aforesaid, if free, shall become a servant for and during the term of seven years; and if a servant, shall finish the time of servitude together with the damages that shall accrue to such person to whom she is a servant, by occasion of any child or children begotten as aforesaid, in the time of her servitude as aforesaid, and after such satisfaction made, shall again become a servant for and during the term of seven years aforesaid; and if the begetter of such a child be a free negro, shall become a servant for and during the term of seven years as aforesaid, to be adjudged by the two next Justices of the Peace where such act is committed, to the party aggrieved; and the issues or children of such unnatural and inordinate copulation shall be servants until they arrive at the age of the male twenty one years, and the females eighteen years, from the time of their birth. And any white man that shall beget any negro woman with child, whether free or servant, shall undergo the same penalties as white women. All which times of servitude by this Act imposed upon the persons having so offended, to be disposed of or employed as the Governour and Council shall think fit, the produce thereof shall be appropriated towards the relief of the poor of the parish wherein the said offence was committed.

"XXII. And as it is customary in other of his Majesty's Colonies in America to make allowances of cloathing to servants at the expiration of their servitude, *Be it enacted* by the authority aforesaid, that every man servant shall at such time of expiration of their servitude as aforesaid, have allowed and given to him, one new hat, a good coat and breeches, either of kersey or broad cloth, one new shirt of white linnen, one new pair of shoes and stockings; and all women-servants, at the expiration of their servitude as aforesaid, shall have allowed and given them a waistcoat and petticoat of new half-thicks or pennistone, a new shift of white linnen, a new pair of shoes and stockings, a blue apron and two caps of white linnen.

"XXIII. *And be it further enacted* by the authority aforesaid, That if any manner of dispute ariseth between masters and their servants, either in relation to their indenture, contracts, wages, freedoms, or any other matter of difference, not herein provided for, it shall be heard and determined by any two Justices of the Peace, saving the right of appeal of either party to the Governour and Council, and if such appeal prove vexatious, it shall be lawful for the Governour and Council to order such costs and damages to the party injured by such appeal, either by servitude by the servant appealing without reason, or such sums of money as they shall think reasonable, by the master or mistress wrongfully appealing, the defendant to be summoned and not condemned unheard.

"XXIV. *And be it further enacted* by the authority aforesaid, That one Act of Assembly of this Province entitled an Act inhibiting the Trading with Servants and Slaves, ratified in open Assembly the sixteenth day of March, one thousand six hundred and ninety-five and six, so far as relates to or concerns servants, be from and immediately after the ratification of this Act, declared null and void, and that part of the said Act is hereby declared void and repealed,

"Ratified in open Assembly, the 11th day of November, A. D. 1717."

SIGNATURES.

APPENDIX II

An Act for the Better Governing and Regulating White Servants, and to Repeal a Former Act Entitled "An Act for the better governing and regulating White Servants"

See III. Cooper, pp. 621-29.

(This Act of 1744 remained the statutory provision throughout the balance of the colonial period, being the text upon which Simpson's "Justice of the Peace"—pub'd. in 1761—was based.)

* * *

"Whereas, the laws hitherto provided in this Province for governing and regulating white servants have proved ineffectual, we pray your most sacred Majesty that it may be enacted,

"I. *And be it enacted,* by his Excellency James Glen, Captain General, Governor, and Commander-in-chief in and over your Majesty's Province of South Carolina, by and with the advice and consent of your Majesty's honorable Council and the Assembly of the said Province, and by the authority of the same, That where any person or persons are imported into this Province without being under contract or indenture, and are unable or unwilling to pay for their passages, it shall and may be lawful, for the importer or importers of such person or persons, before any one of his Majesty's justices of the peace within this Province, to take an indenture or indentures, executed under the hand and seal of such person or persons in consideration of such passage money, . . .[service as in No. 383] which indenture or indentures shall be as binding and effectual in law as if the same had been executed before the arrival of such person or persons in this Province. And if such person or persons shall refuse to execute such indenture or indentures, or to pay his or her passage money, it shall and may be lawful for the importer or importers, after the expiration of twenty days from such refusal, to carry such person or persons before any two justices of the peace, who are hereby impowered and required, upon due examination of all circumstances, to certify, by an instrument in writing, under their hands and seals, the time such person or persons shall be obliged

[119]

to serve such importer or importers, in proportion to the value of the passage, and regard being had to the trade or occupation of such servant or servants; which certificate is hereby declared to be sufficient in law to bind every such person according to the tenor thereof, and to be transferrable, in as full and ample manner as if an indenture had been voluntarily executed in the manner hereinbefore directed."

The certificate of freedom, provided for in section I, of the Act of 1717, appears in a separate section, as No. IX, in this Act. Some significance may attach to the use of the terms importer or importers, and recognition of the value of handicraftsmen is made, in this latter Act. Otherwise, there is no important change.

II. provides, as in 1717, for the case of servants coming from other colonies, and adds to the stipulation that they shall complete their servitude, according to the tenor of their indentures, the further proviso "always, that the consent of such servant to be brought into this Province, and not being a convict, shall be certified on the back of the indenture, under hand and seal, by any one justice of the peace in the colony from whence such servant is brought."

III. adds "except convicts" and omits "or any of the Lords Proprietors deputies" (the colony now being a royal province), as the alternate authority before whom, as well as the Governor, servants may be brought for decision as to terms of service.

IV. is identical with that in the former Act.

V. has a few slight changes, in phrasing only.

VI. the penalty against one who trades unlawfully with servants is changed from "ten pounds current" to "two pounds proclamation money" fine and adds "full costs of suit." Likewise, this fine is to be recovered within "three months" instead of "twenty-five days," as in 1717.

VII. reads "if any servant" lay violent hands on his master &c, whereas the earlier Act says "any servant or hired labourer."

VIII. reflects in this amendment a greater degree of severity in dealing with runaway servants, but also sets a limit to the time that may be added as penalty. The Act of 1717 provides that such servants "shall satisfy or pay . . . all such costs and charges as shall be laid out and expended for their taking up, by servitude." The amended clause reads "for taking up, whipping, and bringing home such servant or servants, by a further and additional servitude, provided the whole time of such additional servitude does not exceed one year after the expiration of the first servitude for absenting as aforesaid." (The maximum for this latter was two years added service. A greater mede of discretion is given the justices; the following addition is made: "which said justices of the peace are thereupon hereby authorized and required to pass judgment for the time such servant or servants shall serve for absence and charges, or either of them, as aforesaid, which judgment, certified under the hands and seals of such justices, is hereby declared to be sufficient in law to bind every such servant or servants according to the tenor thereof, and to be transferable, in as full and ample manner as if indenture or indentures had been voluntarily executed by such servant or servants; provided always, that every party who may think him, her or themselves aggrieved by the judgment of such justices, may and shall have a right of appeal from such judgment to the Governour and council of this Province for the time being, who are hereby authorized to confirm or reverse such judgment or judgments, upon due examination and proof of all circumstances, as to them shall seem meet."

IX. substitutes "twenty shillings proclamation money" for "two pounds current money" as the penalty for entertaining a servant who has no certificate of freedom. If the amount is not over four pounds, recovery shall be made as for small and mean causes. If the total runs over that amount, "by action of debt, bill, plaint, or information, in any court of record in this Province, wherein no session, protection, or wager of law shall be allowed." Also, in case of forged certificates of freedom, only those shall be excused from fine who shall entertain such servant "ignorantly." After the phrase "the pillory &c," is added, "provided the said punishment does not extend to life or member."

X. "twenty shillings current" instead of "two pounds proclamation" money. While the subject matter of these last two sections is somewhat reversed in this later statute, it covers the same ground as the corresponding sections of the Act of 1717. Section XI, of Act 383, is omitted in the present Act. It made further provision to safeguard against the employment of those who might still be under contract, as follows: *"And be it further enacted by the authority aforesaid, That if any freeman shall by any contract agree with any* person or persons, and before the time agreed for be accomplished shall depart to another, he shall perform the tenor of his contract first made and pay the apparent damages that shall arise from his breach of covenant, and shall after that is satisfied be liable to the payment of what damages any other contractor with him shall recover of him by law; and whosoever shall employ any free person (handicraft tradesmen excepted) without a certificate from the last employer, of the performance of his or their last bargain or contract, shall forfeit twenty-five pounds, to be recovered by action of debt, in any court of record in this Province, by the person suffering thereby."

XI. Provides for the satisfaction of servants injured by their masters, corresponding to XIII of the Act of 1717. The amendment reflects an advance, in behalf of the servants. The former proviso considered the penalties for three offences by the master: 1st, admonishment by the Justice of the Peace; 2d, a fine not to exceed ten pounds; 3d, sale of the balance of the servant's time. The amended form provides that the Justice, having found "by lawful proof that the said servant's complaint is just, is hereby impowered and required, under the penalty of five pounds proclamation money, by warrant under his hand and seal, directed to the next constable, to levy and distrain of the goods and chattels of such master or mistress, any sum not exceeding four pounds proclamation money, to be disposed of for the use of the poor of the parish where such offence is committed; and for the second offence, any two justices of the peace shall, and are hereby authorized and required, under the penalty of five pounds proclamation money, each, by instrument in writing under their hands and seals, to make an order directed to any constable, to sell and dispose of the remaining time of service of such servant . . . " continues, as the Act of 1717, and adds: "provided such appeal [*i. e.,* to the Governour and Council] be lodged in the Secretary's office within twenty days from the sentence given by such justices."

XII. Adds "victualler" to "punch-house keeper and vintner," as among those who may not entertain servants, changes the penalty from "forty shillings" to "not exceeding four pounds," and adds: "one moiety to the use of the poor of the parish where such offence is committed, and the other moiety to such person or persons as shall inform and sue for the same." This is Section XIV of the Act of 1717.

XIII. *And be it further enacted* by the authority aforesaid, That from and after the passing of this Act, no servant or servants whatsoever within this Province, shall travel by land or water above two miles from the place of his, her, or their residence without a note, under the hand of his, her, or their master, mistress, or overseer, expressing a permission for such servant or servants so travelling; and if any servant or servants shall, after the passing of this Act, be found above two miles from the place of his, her, or their residence, without such note, he, she, or they shall be deemed and taken as fugitive servant and servants, and shall suffer such penaltys and punishments as by this Act are provided against runaway servants." This perhaps covers section XII of the former Act which made running away in company with a slave a felony.

XIV. Deals with the taking up and custody of runaway servants, being an elaboration of the XVth section under Act 383, which was not properly adequate to the situation. The amended section reads "And for the better discovering, apprehending, securing, and punishing fugitive servants, *Be it further enacted* by the authority aforesaid, That every free person within this Province shall have power, and is hereby authorized, to apprehend any person or persons suspected to be fugitive servant or servants, and shall forthwith conduct such suspected person to the next justice of the peace, who is hereby authorized and required to examine and inquire, in the best manner he can, whether such suspected person is really a fugitive servant or not, and if by confession or otherwise, it shall appear that such person is a fugitive servant, the said justice shall immediately order such servant to be whipped, not exceeding twenty stripes, and shall deliver the said servant to the constable of the parish where the said justice resides, with orders to convey the said servant to his master, mistress, or overseer, if living within the said parish, or otherwise to the constable of the next adjoining parish, who is hereby authorized and required to receive such servant, and immediately to convey him or her, to his or her master, mistress, or overseer, if living within the parish where such last mentioned constable until such servant or servants shall be brought to his or her master, resides, and so on from constable to constable, and parish to parish, mistress, or overseer; but if it shall be doubtful whether such suspected person is really a servant or not, then, and in such case, such suspected person shall be conveyed from constable to constable of the respective parishes through which such suspected person is brought, until he or she shall arrive at Charlestown, where such suspected person shall be delivered to the warden of the work house, who is hereby authorized and required to receive such suspected person into his work house, and to keep him, her or them to hard labour therein for the space of thirty days; and at the time of bringing such person to the work house as aforesaid, the warden is hereby required to publish in the Gazette for three weeks successively, an account of such persons so brought, giving the best description he can of their persons, and unless such person can, within such time prove him, her, or themselves to be free, to the satisfaction of any one of his Majesty's justices of the peace, or shall pay the charges of his, her, or their being brought to the said work house, and of his, her, or their detainer there, and of the said advertisement, such person, at the end of such thirty days, shall be whipped on the bare back, not exceeding twenty lashes, and be turned out of the said work house."

XV. *And be it enacted* by the authority aforesaid, That every free person within this Province intending to travel, may apply to any one of his Majesty's justices of the peace, to whom such free person is known, for a certificate of such freedom and passport, expressing such intention to travel, which certificate and passport every justice of the peace is hereby required to deliver to such free person demanding the same, under his hand and seal, without taking any fee or reward for the same."

XVI. *And be it further enacted* by the authority aforesaid, That within six months next after the passing of this Act, every person keeping a ferry within this Province, shall provide one free white man constantly to attend the same, and on failure thereof, shall forfeit for every month he shall so neglect to provide such free white man, four pounds proclamation money, for the use of such person and persons as shall inform and prosecute for the same, to be recovered on conviction, upon the oath of one or more credible witnesses, before any one justice of the peace, by warrant of distress and sale of the offender's goods."

XVII. *And be it further enacted* by the authority aforesaid, That every free white man attending such ferrys shall be and is hereby authorized and required to examine and apprehend all suspected persons whatsoever, endeavouring to cross such ferry where he shall so attend, and to carry such suspected person or persons before the next justice of the peace, to be dealt with according to the directions of this Act; and in case of refusal or resistance by such suspected person, to command all such persons as he shall think needful, to aid and assist in apprehending and carrying the said suspected person to the said justice."

XVIII. *And be it further enacted* by the authority aforesaid, That every person keeping a ferry within this Province, who shall, after the passing of this Act, transport, or suffer to be transported over such ferry, any servant not having a note or certificate, as herein is before directed, shall forfeit for every such offence four pounds proclamation money, to the use of the owner of such servant, to be recovered upon conviction on the oath of one or more credible witnesses before any one justice of the peace by warrant of distress and sale of the offender's goods."

XIX. *And be it further enacted* by the authority aforesaid, That the several justices of the peace, officers, and other persons required and directed to put this Act in execution, shall be, and are hereby empowered to take and receive for their respective trouble and services therein, the several fees limited and ascertained in the following table, that is to say, to a justice of the peace before whom an indenture is executed, one shilling; for the justice's certificate of service upon refusal to execute an indenture, two shillings and six pence; to the Governour, for the certificate of the age of each servant, five shillings; to the justices if certified by them, two shillings and six pence; to the justices, for an order on conviction of each servant's laying violent hands on his master, mistress, or overseer, two shillings and six pence each; to the justices for passing judgment for a further time of servitude on each servant, two shillings and six pence each; to the Governour for his decree on an appeal from the justices, five shillings; for a reward to the person apprehending each servant, one pound, and three pence per mile to the justice's house; to the justice of the peace before whom a servant is brought, for examining the matter and order thereon, two shillings; to the constable for whipping each servant, four shillings; to the constable per mile from the place where he receives to the place where he delivers each servant, besides ferriage and diet, three pence;

to the marshal or warden of the work house, for receiving and discharging each servant, two shillings and six pence; to the marshal or warden for whipping each servant, two shillings; to diet per diem for each servant, allowing at least a pound of bread and a pound of flesh, wholesome provisions, one shilling and three pence."

XX. *And be it further enacted* by the authority aforesaid, That the several fees hereinbefore limited shall be paid by the masters, mistresses, or overseers of fugitive servants to the constables delivering such servants to them respectively, or to the warden of the work house in Charlestown, if any such servants shall be brought thither, and after such delivery the said warden, constable, and constables, shall be liable to pay on demand such part of the said fees as belong to the other persons concerned in putting this Act in execution to such person or persons respectively, under the penalty of forfeiting double the sum so belonging to such other person or persons, to be recovered by the party grieved, according to the directions of an additional Act to an Act intitled an Act for the tryal of small and mean causes."

XXI. *And be it further enacted* by the authority aforesaid, That the warden of the work house in Charlestown for the time being, shall, within ten days after he receives any fugitive servant, publish the same, at the charge of the owner of such servant, in the Carolina Gazette; and if the said warden shall neglect so to do, he is hereby made liable to the same fines and penalty as persons unlawfully entertaining fugitive servants are by virtue of this Act; and if the said warden shall suffer any fugitive servant so brought to him to escape before he or she is duly delivered to his or her master or mistress, or his or her assigns, then, and in such case, the said warden shall, and is hereby declared to be liable to an action at common law, to be brought at the suit of the party injured, his or her executors or administrators, provided the said action be commenced within six months after the escape of such servant."

XXII. The same as section XVI of the Acts of 1717, except that it provides punishment by the first constable into whose hands the runaway is delivered, "not exceeding twenty-one lashes," by the second and others following "not exceeding seven lashes." The former Act provides this treatment for servants running away "more than twice," while the present provision is for all servants who "shall offend more then once in running away."

XXIII. The same as section XVII of the Act of 1717, except that present provision limits the total punishment to be inflicted upon the servant, in lieu of the fine to be paid in a like case by a freeman, to "thirty-nine lashes." The general provision of the section is for the infliction of nine lashes for every twenty shillings fine.

XXIV. Identical, except wording, with section XVIII of the former Act.

XXV. The general provision for fining masters turning away sick servants &c is the same as in section XIX of Act 383, save the use of the term "proclamation" instead of "current" money. Instead of the latter part of the section providing, as in the earlier statute, against the abuse of privilege by servants wilfully contracting disease or molesting masters with unjust complaints, there is now submitted "and in case any person who is the owner of any servant or servants who shall be committed by virtue of this Act shall suffer him or them to remain in the common gaol, or work house, shall be liable to pay the fees and charges occasioned by such commitment to the marshal or warden respectively, to be recovered as by this Act is directed."

The sections providing penalties for mésalliances, viz numbers XX and XXI of the Act of 1717, do not appear in the present Act.

XXVI. Provides for men servants at the expiration of their time, "two new shirts of coarse white linnen" instead of "one new shirt of white linnen"; and for the women "a waistcoat and petticoat of new halfthicks or coarse plains, two new shifts of white linnen, &x" instead of "a waistcoat and petticoat of new half-thicks or pennistone, a new shift of white linnen &x." Otherwise the same articles for both, as in section XXII of the former Act.

XXVII. Identical with section XXIII of Act 383.

XXVIII. *And be it further enacted* by the authority aforesaid, That no white servant or servants shall hereafter be obliged to appear or serve at any muster or musters of the militia of this Province, or on patrols, except in times of alarms, invasions, or insurrections, any law, usage or custom to the contrary in any wise notwithstanding."

XXIX. General issue may be pleaded and this Act given in evidence.

XXX Repeals the Act of 1717, as former section XXIV does previous Acts.   SIGNATURES.

APPENDIX III

Statistics on Population, Importation of Negro Slaves and Exportation of Rice

Since rice and negro slaves played such a dominant part in the development of the tide-water region, statistics relative to each commodity offer an almost yearly index to the evolution of South Carolina as a colony and as a State.

In the early days, negroes were brought in a few at a time, as were the white servants. The Warrants for Land Grants (1692-1711) note on 55 to 92 grants for the immigrant, his servants and his slaves. The number of the latter varies from one to twelve.

The first comprehensive approach to a census appears under date of September 17th, 1708, when Richard Beresford, one of the agents for the colony, reported that there were:

1,360 free white men
  900 free white women
   60 white servant men
   60 white servant women
1,700 free white children, a total white population of 4,080.

1,800 negro men slaves
1,100 negro women slaves
1,200 Negro children slaves, a total of negro slaves—4,100.

----

  500 Indian men slaves
  600 Indian women slaves
  300 Indian children slaves, a total of Indian slaves—1,400.

Total population ....9,580.[1]

Governor Johnson reported (Jan. 12th, 1719-20): "Tis computed by the Muster Roles & other Observations that at present we may have about 1,600 Fighting men—Computacon of 4 Persons in each Family, the whole of the Whites are 6,400."[2] Feb. 22d,

1717, the "memorial of Joseph Boone and Richard Berresford, Agents, stated that the 'Number of Men is very small that are fitt to bear Arms not 700.' " [3] The Yamassee Indian War may partly explain this apparent drop in numbers from those shown in 1708. Aug. 23d, 1720, Joseph Boone, agent, reported "The Number of White Inhabit.[ts] have been lately computed at 9,000 souls. And the number of Blacks at 12,000."[4] Three years later it was estimated that there were 9,100 slaves. This was based on the amount of tax set up for the year Sept. 29, 1723 to Sept. 29th, 1724.[5] An address to the King (July 23d, 1730) concerning Purry's plans refers to Carolina "where there are not at present above 3,000 White Families."[6] August 26th, 1754, Gov. Glen reported, "85,000 bbls of rice from Charles Town since the first of November last; 2,000 negroes imported ditto—and sold @ 250, 260, 270 £ currency and women @ 200." [7]

Nov. 21st, 1745, in connection with a plea for the export of rice to *any* foreign port, it was 'computed' that there were "10,000 White Inhabitants Men, Woman and Children and 'known' about 40,000 negroes."[8]

In volume XII of the London Transcripts (p. 180), appears the following statement: "Carolina. A List of Negro's Imported from May 30th, 1721 to September 29th, 1726:

From May 30th to September 29th, 1721 ...... 104 Negro's
" Sept. 29th to Sept. 29th, 1722 215
" " " 1722 to Sept. 29th, 1723 527
" " " 1723 to " " 1724 602
" " " 1724 to " " 1725 433
" " " 1725 to " " 1726 1,751
_____

Total since His Excellency's Govern't. 3,632
Port of Charles Town
Wm. Hammerton
So. Carolina
In Councell this 18th day of Jany 1726/7.
Sworn before me Ar: Middleton."

In the Supplement to the Gazette of Dec. 8th, 1759, is printed the following:

"Imports at Charles-Town, for Twelve Years, beginning the 24th June, 1747:

Slaves

1749—   72
1750—   442
1751—   914
1752—1,560
1753— 661   The Gazette of May 31st, 1773 states that "The
1754—3,648   whole Quantity of Slaves Imported from the 1st of
1755—1,305   January, 1753, to the 1st of January, 1773 is 43,965."
1756—2,239   Also "the greatest quantity in any one year was 7,184
1757—1,207   in 1765, which is 4,457 less than arrived the present
1758—2,477   year."
1759—1,957

A letter from a South Carolina merchant, May 1st, 1735, states that " about ten days since a Ship from Angola arrived with 318 Slaves." The further advice is vouchsafed that other vessels expected will make "a great number of Negroes this year." (L. T.-No. 17, p. 349). A letter to the Gazette (printed in the issue of March 9th, 1738) refers to "such large Importations of 2,600 or 2,800 Negroes every year."

The following page reflects the difficulty of making any adequate statement such as one might expect in census figures. Items appear, as there noted, as to white men, women and children; the same for negro slaves; the same for Indian slaves. At the expense of some duplication, the reports on the importation of slaves have been set up by years. This feature presents a fairly adequate picture. The attempt to work in numbers as to whites is far less adequate. Finally there is appended Gov. Johnson's report to the Board of Trade (Jan. 12th, 1719-20), reflecting his estimates of the various Indian nations.

Slaves and Rice

Sir John Yeamans "brought with him from Barbados his negro slaves, their first introduction into Carolina.[9] The Records of the Secretary of the Province disclose the intent that by "150 acres of land for every able man Servant in that we means Negros as well as Christians."[10] That land was so granted is attested by Warrants. Aug. 17th, 1694 to Aug. 15th, 1695 sixteen owners were granted 50 acres each for a total of 69 negroes whom they brought in.[11] In 1708, as above noted, there were 4,100 negroes in the colony.[12]

"Twenty barrels of rice, according to a Gazette contributor, would represent the average yield of a plantation worked by seven slaves."

The following does not purport to be a complete list of slave importations. But items shown reflect the interrelation of slaves, rice and white servants.

year	no. slaves imported	bbls. rice exported		year	no. slaves imported	bbls. rice exported
1706 —	24			1722 —	323*	— 23,559 bbls.
1707 —	22	June 6, 1712 to		1723 —	436*	— 20,151 bbls.
1708 —	53	June 6, 1713		1724 —	604*	— 13,980 bbls.
1709 —	107	there was ex		1725 —	433*	— 17,734 bbls.
1710 —	131	ported 12,677		1726 —	1,751*	— 23,031 bbls.
1711 —	170	bbls., and 200		1727 —		— 26,884 bbls.
1712 —	76	bags of rice.		1728 —		— 29,905 bbls.
1713 —	159	(L.T., VI.,		1729 —		— 32,384 bbls.
1714 —	419	p. 173.)		1730 —		— 41,722 bbls.
1715 —	81			1731 —		— 39,487 bbls.
1716 —	67			1732 —		— 37,068 bbls.
1717 —	573			1733 —		— 50,726 bbls.
1718 —	529			1734 —		— 30,323 bbls.
1719 —	541			1735 —		— 45,317 bbls.
1720 —	601	— 13,623 bbls.		1736 —		— 52,349 bbls.[14]
1721 —	165*	— 21,879 bbls.				and 1,554 bags.

Several comparisons of longer periods than one year, may serve to accentuate the picture. Rice exported in the period from 1720 to 1729—264,488 bbls. 1730-1739—499,525 [13] bbls. As only 1/15th was consumed in Gt. Brit. and her dominions, the restriction on export was extremely onerous.

year	no. slaves imported	bbls. rice exported		year	no. slaves imported	bbls. rice exported
1748 —		— 50,745 bbls.		1754 —	3,648	— 69,925 bbls.
1749 —	72	— 51,526 bbls.		1755 —	1,305	— 95,813 bbls.
1750 —	442	— 45,887 bbls.		1756 —	2,239	— 72,373 bbls.
1751 —	914	— 52,663 bbls.		1757 —	1,207	— 65,647 bbls.
1752 —	1,560	— 81,868 bbls.		1758 —	2,477	— 56,812 bbls.
1753 —	661	— 48,089 bbls.		1759 —	1,957	— 75,463 bbls.[15]

For the years 1721 to 1726, 3,632 slaves were imported; 120,334 bbls. of rice were exported. Thirty years later (1751-1756), 10,327 slaves were imported; 420,731 bbls. of rice were exported. Three times as many slaves; three and one half times as much rice.

Not everyone in the colony was complacent about this situation. Under date of March 9th, 1738, the Gazette published the following contribution from a subscriber:

"I cannot avoid observing that altho' a few Negroes annually imported into this Province might be an advantage to most People; yet such large Importations of 2,600 or 2,800 Negroes every Year is not only a Loss to many, but in the End may prove the Ruin of the Province, as it most certainly does that of many poor industrious Planters, who unwarily engage in buying more than they have Occasion for, or are able to pay. It is for their Sakes only I now take the Trouble of writing this, that they may not further involve themselves in utter ruin.

"Negroes may be said to be the Bait proper for catching a Carolina Planter, as certain as Beef to catch a Shark. How many under the Notion of 18 Months Credit, have been tempted to buy more Negroes than they could possibly expect to pay in 3 Years! . . . If I may be so bold as to give my Advice in the Affair of Negroes, it would be this, that before any Planter offer to buy one more, or even to venture into a Negro Yard, he should first make up an Account of all he owes now to every Person, and then make a Calculation of what he may reasonably expect to make this Year. . . . Suppose a Man has 20 Negroes, and for these 4 Years past has made in all 240 Barrels of Rice, he may expect to have 60 Barrels next Year, which at a Medium of Price will be about 700 £ Currency . . . if the . . . Man finds he owes only 100 £ he may safely buy 2 Negroes, and have a common Chance to pay them besides his annual Charges. . . . Were it possible to prevent any Negroes to be imported for 3 Years to come, I am perswaded it would be for the general Advantage of all the Inhabitants in this Province, and the only Means to relieve us from the Load of Debts we are now owing to Great Britain, which I believe is equal to the Amount of 3 Years Produce."

Miscellaneous Statistics Showing Estimates of Population, as Evidenced in the Various Sources, Drawn on for Material.

	White Inhabitants		
	Men	Women	Children
Arrivals since 1st Fleet, to Jan. 20th, 1671-2	337	71	62
reduced to this date to [16]	278	69	59
9/11/1708 [17]	1,360-F.	900-F.	1,177-F.
	1,800	1,100	1,200
	500-Sl.	600-Sl.	300-Sl.
		60-S.	60-S.

2/22/1717, fit to bear arms ....700 [white men].[18]

3/28/1720 ....about 9,000 whites.[19]

1/12/1719-20 ....6,400 whites.[20]

9/ 8/1721 ....9,000 whites.—12,000 Blacks.[21]

7/23/1730 ...."above 3,000 white families".[22]

7/17/1736 ....15,000 white inhabitants.[23]

11/21/1745 ....10,000 whites—40,000 negroes.[24]

7/ 9/1749 ....25,000 whites—39,000 negroes.[25]

12/ 2/1756 .... 5,000 or 6,000 men on the muster rolls—

(age 16 to 60).[26]

11/30/1770 ....in Charleston 5,030 whites—5,830 Blacks.

Total in colony ....75,178 Blacks.[27]

Reference has been made to Indian relations on the frontier, and to the fact that members of Indians appear as slaves, Jan. 12th, 1719-20, Col. Johnson reported to the Board of Trade, his estimates re the various Indian nations:

Distance from Charles Town	Name	Villages	Men	Total
90-S.W.	—Yamasses	10	413	1,215
130-S.W.	—Apalatchicolas	2	64	214
140-W.	—Apalachees	4	275	638
150-W. by N.	—Savanas	3	67	283
180-W.N.W.	—Euchees	2	130	400
250-W. by N.	—Ochesees, or Creeks	10	731	2,406
440-W.	—Abikaws	15	502	1,773
430-S.W. by W.	—Albamas	4	214	770
390-W.S.W.	—Tallibooses	13	636	2,343
200—N.N.W.	—Catapaws	7	570	1,470
170-N.	—Sarows	1	140	510

Distance from Charles Town	Name	Villages	Men	Total
100-N.E.	—Waccomassus	4	210	610
200-N.E.	—Cape Fears	5	76	206
70-N.	—Santees	2	43 ⎫	125
100-N.	—Congarees	1	22 ⎬	
80-N.E.	—Wensawa	1	36	106
60-N.E.	—Seawees	1	57 W&Ch	57
Mixt. wth ye	English ⎱ —Itwans	1	80	240
Settlement.	⎰ —Corsaboys	5	95	295
	The Cherokees (Vizt)			
450-N.W.	—The upper Settlement	19	900 ⎫	
390-N.W.	—The middle Settlement	30	2,500 ⎬	11,530
320-N.W.	—The lower Settlement	11	600 ⎭	
640-W.	—The Chikesaws	6	700	1,900

(*LT*, VII, pp. 238-9.)

NOTES FOR APPENDIX III

[1] *LT*, V, p. 203. B.P.R.O. Proprietors-B.T., vol. 9, p. 82.

[2] *LT*, VII, pp. 233-4. B.P.R.O. Proprietors-B.T., vol. 10, 2.201.

[3] *Ibid.*, p. 7. B.P.R.O. Proprietors-B.T., vol. 10, 2.111.

[4] *LT*, VIII, p. 66. B.P.R.O. South Carolina-B.T., vol. I.

[5] *JCHA*, No. 6, p. 431.

[6] *LT*, XVIII, p. 89.

[7] *LT*, XXVI. B.P.R.O. South Carolina-B.T., vol. 18, K-99, p. 112.

[8] *LT*, XXII, p. 115.

[9] McCrady, I, p. 151.

[10] Records of the Secretary of the Province, p. 18.

[11] Warrants (1692-1711), pp. 55 to 92.

[12] *LT*, V, p. 203.

[13] Chapman J. Milling: "Colonial South Carolina," p. 88.

[14] Schaper: AHA (1900), I, 316.

[15] *Gazette* of August 8th, 1759.

[16] Secretary Dalton's report to Lord Ashley (Cal. St. Pap., VII, p. 736).

[17] Computation of inhabitants, or report to Lords Proprietors (*LT*, No. 5, p. 203).

[18] Memorial of colony agents (*LT*, No. 7, p. 7).

[19] Answer to Lords Commissioners (*Ibid.*, p. 255).

[20] Gov. Johnson's report (*LT*, No. 7, pp. 233-4; and pp. 238-9).

[21] Report to the King (*LT*, No. 9, pp. 67-8; *also Ibid.*, No. 8, p. 66).

[22] Report to the King (*LT*, No. 14, p. 243).

[23] Report to the King (*Ibid.*, No. 18, p. 89).

[24] Agent's report (*LT*, No. 22, p. 115).

[25] Computation from muster rolls (*LT*, No. 27, pp. 369-70).

[26] Computation from muster rolls (*LT*, No. 27, p. 192).

[27] Wm. Bull to Sec'y of State for America (*LT*, No. 32, pp. 388 and 395).

APPENDIX IV

*Complete List of White Servants Appearing as Items in the
Wills and Inventories Recorded in Probate Court of
Charleston County*

July 30th, 1681—Est. Rich. Banks: Rights of servitude in four
servants:
1 man and 1 woman .... £ 19.
2 young men .... £ 25.
(vol. 1672-1692, p. 85).
Sept. 16th, 1682—Est. John Horton: One sick servt. maid.. £   6.6
(*ibid.*, p. 110).
Feby. 13th, 1683—Est. John Smyth: Two white servants 19
months to serve .... £   8.
(*ibid.*, p. 21).
June 9th, 1718—Est. John Fulford: To one white Servt. man. £ 40.
(vol. 1711-1718., p. 80).
(*no date*)—Will of John Green: Balance of John Weaver's
time, in lieu of .... £150.
(vol. 1722-1724, p. 220).
April 22nd, 1724—Est. George Ford: To one white man .... £ 20.
(*ibid.*, p. 280).
May 27th, 1724—Est. Major Pawley: 1 white servt. 3 years
to serve .... £ 30.
(*ibid.*, p. 292).
Sept. 3, 1724—Est. Col. Barnwell: 13 Years of a bought
Servant .... £ 50.
(vol. 1724-1725, p. 43).
June 30th, 1726—Est. Madm. Willoughby Gibbes: A white
servants time .... £ 50.
(vol. 1732-1736, p. 90).
Aug. 30th, 1727—Will of Richard Wigg: Item. I give unto my
said Son Thomas Wigg my servant man John to be his
Servant during the remainder of his time which he hath to
serve me.
(vol. 1671-1727, p. 295).

(*no date*)—Est. Sherriff: A White Servant sold .... £ 65.
(vol. 1722-1726, p. 278).
Aug. 23, 1732—Est. John Arnold:
 1 White Servant woman .... £ 25.
 1 White servant woman .... £ 10.
(vol. 1731-1736, p. 487).
Apr. 10th, 1733—Est. Thomas Boone: 1 White Servant Man
 Three years to Serve .... £ 20.
(vol. 1732-1736, p. 19).
Apr. 20th, 1733—Est. Jonathan Main: 3 Years Service of a
 White woman (Nanny) .... £ 50.
(*ibid.*, p. 42).
Oct. 15th, 1734—Est. Thomas Bolling: To a wite servant
 garl .... £ 60.
(*ibid.*, p. 128).
Dec. 9th, 1734—Est. Richard Basden: To thre months Serv-
 vice of an aprentice .... £ 20.
(vol. 1732-1736, 135).
Feby. 19th, 1736—Est. John Jameson: of his (Patrick Blair
 of St. Christie) two daughters Ann Blair and Isabella Blair
 Dr their two Indentures £5 each is short £10 at 775 .... £77.10
(Vol. 1732-1746, p. 1).
 These apparently have to do with apprentices.
Feby. 22d., 1736—Est. John Jameson: By John Bedon for
 said Flemins son—Johns Indentures £38.15
(vol. 1732-1746, p. 1).
Dec. 5th, 1738—Est. Alexander Kilpatrick: A white servants
 Time .... £ 40.
(vol. 1739-1743, p. 5).
Mch. 26th, 1742—Est. Jos. Fidler: 3¾ Years service of an
 Indented Shoemaker .... £ 60.
(vol. 1741-1743, p. 168).
October, 1742—Est. John Sikes: A white Servant Maid over
 his Indenture Thom. Harding for .... £ 40.
(vol. 1741-1743, p. 207).
June-July, 1743—Est. James St. John:
 A Dutch servant man named Gaspor a shoemaker to serve
 upward a year and half .... £ 50.

A boy Stephen his son to serve upward of ten years .... £ 30.
(vol. 1739-1743, p. 289).

Jany. 1st, 1751—Est. Evan Vaughan: To Servant Woman 2
years to serve .... £ 25.
(vol. 1751-1753, p. 446).

June 25th, 1754—Est. Maj. Wm. Palmers: 3 years time of an
Indented Servant Boy .... £ 40.
(vol. 1753-1756, p. 224).

Aug. 17th, 1754—Est. James Summers: a Servant man having about 2½ years to serve .... £ 60.
(*ibid.*, p. 249).

Feb. 11th, 1755—Est. John Dart: an Indented Dutch boy to
serve 6 Years .... £ 50.
(*ibid.*, p. 298).

Dec. 10th, 1756—Est. Peter Nygh:
A woman servants time about 2 years .... £ 26.
A boys Do about 4 years .... £ 48.
(vol. 1756-1758, p. 8).

Feb. 3rd, 1757—Est. Solom Isaac: 2 years and 8 months time
of a Dutch Servant man a Cooper .... £ 50.
(*ibid.*, p. 64).

July 30th, 1766—Est. Thos. Scott:
Servant man .... £ 175.
Servant girl .... £ 50.

Sept. 21, 22, 1767—Est. Benj. Backhouse: The Remaining
part of Dennis McCarthys Time being an indented Servant. £ 15.
(*ibid.*, p. 179).

Again, on page 229 of the same volume, is recorded in the
estate of Benjamin Backhouse, Tavern keeper, The Time of an
Irish Servant .... £ 25.

BIBLIOGRAPHY

Primary Sources
(Full names and abbreviations)

Journals of the Commons House of Assembly of the Province of South Carolina; Journals No. 1-39 (1692-1775) ......*J.C.H.A.*

Council Journal; Journals No. 1-38 (1685-1774) ............*C.J.*

Public Records of South Carolina designated as London Transcripts; Volumes 1-36 (1663-1782) ........................*L.T.*

Register of the Province of South Carolina; 1671-1719 (Thirteen Volumes) ......................................*R.P.S.C.*

Probate Court Records (Charleston County); 1672-1779 (Miscellaneous, Wills, Records of various kinds, including those of the "court of Ordinary" ............................*P.C.R.*

Trott, Nicholas. *"The Laws of the Province of South Carolina"*— *Trott MS*

Cooper's Statutes at Large ....*Cooper*

Simpson, William. *The Practical Justice of the Peace and Parish Officer of His Majesty's Province of South Carolina* (Charleston: 1761) ....*Simpson*

Calendar State Papers Colonial-America and West Indies; Volumes I-XVIII ..............................*C.S.P, Colonial*

South Carolina Gazette (1732-1768) ....*Gazette*

Letter Books of Henry Laurens, Merchant (1746-1783) ....*Laurens*

Warrants for Land Grants (1692-1715) ....*Warrants*

Parish Registers:

St. Thomas & St. Denis ....(1693–1778)
St. James, Santee ....(1758–1789)
St. Helena's ....(1740–1793)
St. Andrew's ....(1719–1783)
Christ Church ....(1700–1784)
Prince Frederick (Winyaw) ....(1713–1778)
Episcopal church in Orangeburg and Amelia
Townships ....(1740)

A State of the Province of Georgia, Attested upon Oath in the Court of Savannah, Nov. 10th, 1740 (London: 1742—"Printed for W. Meadows, at the Angel in Cornhill").

Vestry Books:
St. Matthews .... (1767–1838)
St. Helena's (Beaufort) .... (1726–1812)
Christ Church .... (1708–1759)
Prince Frederick (Winyaw) .... (1713–1778)
St. John's (Colleton) .... (1734–1817)
St. Stephen's .... (1754–1802)

Records of the St. Andrew's Society (est'd. 1729)

Records of the General Assembly, Charleston, July 25, 1761 ("Records of the States of the U. S. A., 1761-1775"). Microfilm compilation by the Library of Congress in association with the University of North Carolina; collected and edited under direction of William Sumner Jenkins, 1949.

BIBLIOGRAPHY

Secondary Sources

ANDREWS, CHARLES M. "American Colonial History," *A.Hist.Assn. Reports* (1898).

——————————. "Colonial Commerce," *A.H.Review*, XX.

BACOT, D. HUGER. "Up Country of South Carolina," *A.H.R.*, XXVII.

BALLAGH, JAMES C. "White Servitude in the Colony of Virginia," *Johns Hopkins University Studies (in Historical and Political Science)*, XIII (1895).

——————————. "Introduction to Southern Economic History," chapter on "The Land System," *A.H.A.* (1897).

BARRINGER, LAURENCE SCOTT. *Family Facts for the Future*, Columbia: The R. L. Bryan Company, 1958.

BASSETT, JOHN SPENCER. "Slavery and Servitude in the Colony of North Carolina," *J.H.U.S.*, XIV (1896).

——————————. "Report of the Conference on the Relation of Geography to History," *A.H.A.* (1908), I.

BODDIE, WILLIAM WILLIS. *History of Williamsburg*. Columbia: The State Company, 1923.

BUTLER, JAMES DAVIE. "British Convicts Shipped to American Colonies," *A.H.A.*, IX.

CARPENTER, A. H. "Naturalization in England and the Colonies," *A.H.A.*, IX.

CARROLL, B. R. *Historical Collections of South Carolina*, Vol. II. New York: 1836.

COOKE, JOHN ESTEN. *Virginia, A History of the People*. Boston: Houghton Mifflin Company, 1887.

COOPER, HARRIET C. "James Oglethorpe, the Founder of Georgia," *A.H.R.*, X.

CRANE, VERNER W. *The Southern Frontier, 1670-1732*. Ann Arbor: University of Michigan Press, 1956.

——————————. "The Southern Frontier in Queen Anne's War," *A.H.R.*, XXIV.

CRAVEN, WESLEY F. "The Southern Colonies in the 17th Century," *A History of the South*, I.

DONNAN, ELIZABETH. "The Slave Trade Into South Carolina Before the Revolution," *A.H.R.*, XXXIII (1927-28).

FAUST, A. B. *The German Element in the United States.* Boston: Houghton Mifflin Company, 1909.

————————————. "Swiss Emigration to the American Colonies in the 18th Century," *A.H.R.*, XXII.

FORD, HENRY JONES. *The Scotch Irish in America.* Princeton: Princeton University Press, 1915.

GEISER, KARL F. "Redemptioners and Indentured Servants in the Colony and Commonwealth of Pennsylvania," Supp. to *Yale Review*, X (Aug. 1901).

HANNA, CHARLES A. *The Scotch-Irish in the United States.* New York: A. P. Putnam's Sons, 1902.

HARROWER, JOHN. "Diary of John Harrower," *A.H.R.*, VI.

HIRSCH, ARTHUR HENRY. *The Huguenots of Colonial South Carolina.* Durham: Duke University Press, 1928.

HOOKER, RICHARD J. (ed.). *The Carolina Backcountry on the Eve of the Revolution.* Chapel Hill: University of North Carolina Press, 1953.

HUDNUT, RUTH ALLISON, and CROTHERS, HAYES BAKER. "Acadian Transients in South Carolina," *A.H.R.*, XLIII (1937-38).

JERNEGAN, MARCUS W. "Slavery and the Beginnings of Industrialism in the American Colonies, " *A.H.R.*, XXV.

————————————. "A Forgotten Slavery of Colonial Days," *Harpers* (Oct. 1913).

JERVEY, THEODORE D. "White Indented Servants of South Carolina," *S.C.H. & G. Mag.*, XII (1911).

LOW, A. MAURICE. *The American People: A Study in National Psychology.* Boston: Houghton Mifflin Company, 1911. I.

McCORMAC, EUGENE IRVING. "White Servitude in Maryland," *J.H.U.S.*, XXII (1904).

McCRADY, EDWARD. *The History of South Carolina Under the Proprietary Government, 1670-1719.* New York: The MacMillan Company, 1897.

MERIWETHER, ROBERT L. *The Expansion of South Carolina, 1729-1765.* Kingsport: Southern Publishers, Inc., 1950.

MILLING, CHAPMAN J. (ed). *Colonial South Carolina: Two Contemporary Descriptions, by Gov. James Glen and Dr. George Milligen Johnstone.* Columbia: University of South Carolina Press, 1951.

MORSE, JEDEDIAH. *The American Universal Geography,* Part I.

MOSES, BERNARD. "Colonial Society of America," *A.H.A.* (1911).

OLMSTED, FREDERICK LAW. *A Journey in the Seaboard Slave States.* New York: Dix and Edwards, 1856.

—————————————————. *The Proprietary Province, A.H.R.,* I & II.

—————————————————. *American Colonies in the 17th Century.*

PHILLIPS, ULRICH B. *Life and Labor in the Old South.*

—————————————————. *Plantations and the Frontier.*

—————————————————. "The South Carolina Federalists," *A.H.R.,* XIV.

—————————————————. "Plantations with Slave Labor and Free," *A.H.R.,* XXX.

RAMSAY, DAVID. *The History of South Carolina, From Its First Settlement in 1670 to the Year 1808.* Vol. I. Trenton: 1785.

RAVENEL, HARRIOTT HORRY. *Eliza Pinckney.* New York: Charles Scribner's Sons, 1928.

REVILL, JANIE. *A Compilation of the Original Lists of Protestant Immigrants to South Carolina, 1763-1773.* Columbia: 1939.

SALLEY, A. S. *Warrants for Land Grants.* I, II.

—————————————————. *Journal of the Grand Council of South Carolina.*

—————————————————. "Commissions and Instruction from the Lords Proprietors of Carolina to Public Officials of South Carolina (1685-1715)." (A volume for South Carolina Historical Commission).

SCHAPER, WILLIAM A. "Sectionalism and Representation in South Carolina," *Annual Report of A.H.A. for 1900.* Washington: 1901.

SCHARF. *History of Maryland.*

SMITH, ABBOTT EMERSON. *Colonists in Bondage: White Servitude and Convict Labor in America, 1607-1776.* Chapel Hill: University of North Carolina Press, 1947.

—————————————————. "The Transported Convicts to the American Colonies in the 17th Century," *A.H.R.,* XXXIX.

SMITH, HENRY A. M. "Purrysburgh," *S. C. H. & G. Mag.,* X (Oct. 1909).

————————————. *The Baronies of South Carolina.* Charleston: South Carolina Historical Society, 1931.

SMITH, W. ROY. *South Carolina as a Royal Province, 1719-1776.* New York: The MacMillan Company, 1903.

STONE, A. H. "Some Problems of South Economic History," *A.H.R.,* XIII.

————————————. "Letters of Thos. Newe, from S. C.—1682," *A.H.R.,* XII.

————————————. "South Carolina in the Presidential Election of 1800," *A.H.R.,* IV.

————————————. "Sketch of Pinckney's Plan for a Constitution—1787," *A.H.R.,* IX.

WALLACE, DAVID DUNCAN. *History of South Carolina,* I. New York: American Historical Society, Inc., 1934.

WALSH, RICHARD. *Charleston's Sons of Liberty.* Columbia: University of South Carolina Press, 1959.

VOIGHT, GILBERT P. "The German and German-Swiss Element in South Carolina, 1732-1752," *Bulletin of the University of South Carolina,* No. 113 (Sept. 1922).

NOTE: Names listed in the tables and Appendix IV are not indexed. Spelling of proper names, with few exceptions, conforms to that in the various sources noted, which may differ from the usual rendering, *i. e.* *Gourden* for *Gourdin.*

Aalder, Richard, 86
Acadians, 36-37
Acts and other measures (relating to white servants), 1661, "An Act for the good governing of Servants (Barbados)," 4; 1686, "An Act inhibiting the trading with servants or slaves" (including penalties for absconding servants), 74; April 9, 1687 (provision for servants arriving without indentures), 72; 1691, servant freed if punishment too severe, 80; 1696, "An Act for the Encouragement of the Importation of White Servants," 19; Nov. 3, 1698 (for promoting importation of servants), 19; June 7, 1712 (to foster importation of servants), 28; 1712, fine for importing criminals, 39; 1712 (punishment for petty larceny, 78; June 30, 1716, "An Act for the better Setling and Regulating the Militia" (military service for servants), 32; June 30, 1716, "An Act for the Encouragement of the Importation of White Servants," 19; May 2, 1716, servant killed, 33-34; Aug. 4, 1716 (to pay for 32 white servants purchased by the governor), 29; 1717, "An Act for the Better Governing and Regulating White Servants" (*See* Appendix I); 1717 (provision for servants under 16 years old arriving without indentures) punish-

ment of runaway servants and of those who trade with or harbor runaways), 72, 74, 77, 79; 1717 (every plantation with 10 working hands must have one white servant), 31; June 1722 (tax on Negroes to encourage importation of white servants), 31; April 1725 (penalty for not importing white servants), 31; 1726 (proportioning white servants to slaves), 31; 1727, (proportioning white servants to slaves), 31; 1727, stealing of pettiaugers and slaves by servants, a felony; runaway servants (procedure with runaway servants), 76; 1732, duties on slaves to be used for settlement of poor protestants, 53; 1739 (proportioning of white servants to slaves), 31; May 1740, regulation of patrols, 32; Dec. 1741, patrols, 33; 1741, to prevent importation of criminals, 40; 1744 (penalties for running away and provision for certificates of release, penalties for masters' severity), 75-76, 81; 1745, patrols, 33; 1746 (provision that masters of all overseers and white servants obliged to do patrol duty must furnish overseers and servants with a horse and furniture), 33; June 14, 1751, funds for white settlers (poor protestants), 63; 1752, measures to induce further settlements of poor protestants, 59; July 25, 1761, additional funds for poor protestants, 65.
Agnen, Alexander and wife, 22
Akerman, Albert (*also* wife and child —no first names given), 69
Alexander, Rich, 4
Allen, Andrew, 28